AMERICAN HERITAGE

August, 1970 · Volume XXI, Number 5

William Ellery

"I am going off the stage of life..."

Death concerns us notably in this issue—the death of a great President (page 8) and the ways in which death strikes all men (see our article on tombstones, page 20). A "lovely and soothing death"—to use Walt Whitman's words—is not accorded to many. Only a felicitous few pass away in quiet repose. One such was William Ellery of Rhode Island, a signer of the Declaration of Independence, who died on February 15, 1820, aged ninety-two. A friend described his death in a letter to the National Gazette and Literary Register, *in the old-fashioned and moving passage below. We learned of it while browsing through Volume XII of that fascinating if obscure work,* Sibley's Harvard Graduates, *written by Clifford K. Shipton for the Massachusetts Historical Society. Ellery was one of thirty members of the Class of 1747.*

"Old Mr. Ellery died like a philosopher. In truth death, in its common form, never came near him. His strength wasted gradually for the last year, until he had not enough left to draw in his breath, and so he ceased to breathe. The day on which he died, he got up as usual and dressed himself, took his old flag bottomed chair, without arms, in which he had sat for more than half a century, and was reading Tully's Offices in the Latin without glasses, though the print was as fine as that of the smallest pocket Bible. Dr. W. stopped in on the way to the Hospital, as he usually did; and on perceiving the old gentleman could scarcely raise his eyelids to look at him, took his hand, and found that his pulse was gone. After drinking a little wine and water, Dr. W. told him his pulse beat stronger. 'O, yes, Doctor, I have a charming pulse. But,' he continued, 'it is idle to talk to me in this way. I am going off the stage of life, and it is a great blessing that I go free from sickness, pain and sorrow.' Some time after, his daughter, finding him become extremely weak, wished him to be put to bed, which he at first objected to, saying he felt no pain, and there was no occasion for his going to bed. Presently after, however, fearing he might possibly fall out of his chair, he told them they might get him upright in bed, so that he could continue to read. They did so, and he continued reading Cicero very quietly for some time; presently they looked at him and found him dead, sitting in the same posture, with his book under his chin, as a man who becomes drowsy and goes to sleep."

AMERICAN HERITAGE

The Magazine of History

SENIOR EDITOR
Bruce Catton

EDITOR
Oliver Jensen

ARTICLES EDITOR: **E. M. Halliday**

ASSOCIATE EDITORS
Nat Brandt · **Barbara Klaw**
Bernard A. Weisberger

ART DIRECTOR: **Chester Prosinski**

COPY EDITOR: **Carol Angell**

ASSOCIATE COPY EDITOR: **Joyce O'Connor**

ASSISTANT EDITORS
Jessica Bourgeois **Carla Davidson**
Mary Dawn Earley

CONSULTING EDITOR: **Joan Paterson Kerr**

CONSERVATION EDITOR: **Anthony Wolff**

ASSOCIATE CONSERVATION EDITOR
Elizabeth N. Layne

CONTRIBUTING EDITOR: **Robert C. Alberts**

PUBLISHER: **Paul Gottlieb**

ADVISORY BOARD
Allan Nevins, *Chairman*

Carl Carmer	Louis C. Jones
Gerald Carson	Alvin M. Josephy, Jr.
Marshall B. Davidson	Howard H. Peckham
John A. Garraty	Francis S. Ronalds
Eric F. Goldman	S. K. Stevens

American Heritage Publishing Co., Inc.

PRESIDENT
James Parton

CHAIRMAN, EDITORIAL COMMITTEE
Joseph J. Thorndike

SENIOR EDITOR FOR BOOK PUBLISHING
Richard M. Ketchum

EDITORIAL ART DIRECTOR: **Murray Belsky**

AMERICAN HERITAGE is published every two months by American Heritage Publishing Co., Inc.; editorial and executive offices, 551 Fifth Avenue, New York, N.Y. 10017. Treasurer, Marjorie C. Dyer; Secretary, John C. Taylor III. Correspondence about subscriptions should be sent to American Heritage Subscription Office, 383 West Center Street, Marion, Ohio 43302. Single copies: $5.00. Annual subscriptions: $20.00 in U.S. and Canada; $21.00 elsewhere.

A ten-year Index covering Volumes VI–XV is available at $5.00; a new five-year Index of Volumes XVI–XX has just been published at $3.50.

AMERICAN HERITAGE will consider but assumes no responsibility for unsolicited materials. Title registered U.S. Patent Office. Second-class postage paid at New York, N.Y., and at additional mailing offices.

Sponsored by
American Association for State & Local History · Society of American Historians

CONTENTS *August, 1970 · Volume XXI, Number 5*

COVER: Austere in life, our Puritan forefathers were often fanciful in death, as the intricately wrought and often long-winded tombstones of New England bear eloquent witness. This is part of the headstone for the Reverend Silas Biglow, who was buried at Paxton, Massachusetts, in 1769, his high calling forever remembered in a stylized relief—arms outthrust in exhortation. More of this same stone is reproduced in our article on "Graven Images," by Avon Neal. Mr. Neal and his wife, Ann Parker, have illustrated it with some of their well-known hand rubbings. *Back Cover:* This charming pair of paintings by George Wright not only make a little joke but show a single railroad-car interior.

A CLEAN BREAK

Something very strange has happened in the United
States very recently. Traditional attitudes and values
that have prevailed and come down from generation to
generation in all but unbroken succession since the
founding of the republic have suddenly been overturned
or are in the process of being overturned. Traditional
American ways of looking at things—including the traditional way of looking at our own past—have suddenly
been reversed. A startling discontinuity, as stark as a
geologic fault, has occurred in our cultural history since
1964.

It is a temptation, and one constantly yielded to by
social commentators, to look upon these things (like the
geologic fault) as having simply *happened*—as having occurred without human volition or control. The environment has changed, it is said; no wonder people and their
attitudes change. The process is made to appear as in-
exorable as changes in the phase of the moon.

What has "happened" in America has been largely
the doing of the older half of our present population—
those born before the Second World War. Through their
ingenuity and enterprise and with the help of their

"In terms of change in American attitudes and American values, these last five years have surely been the crucial ones in the quarter century since V-J Day. And these changes seem of such a magnitude that every American except the very young, the very empty, and the very enclosed must now, to some extent, feel himself a foreigner in his native land"

WITH THE PAST

equally ingenious and enterprising predecessors of the generations before, the members of the present older generation have changed the country so radically that the old conditions under which the old values obtained are simply not there any more. True enough, the change was brought about (in traditional American fashion) entirely without planning, and, indeed, its social effects have by and large not been felt by the generation responsible. Not really understanding what it has wrought (still quaintly anthropomorphizing computers, for example) and being beyond the age when long-held attitudes and values are easily surrendered, the older half of the country mostly clings to the old ideas. In the meantime the younger half, those born since the war, have grown up in a whole new world and, in a triumph of environment over heredity, have become a new breed. The fathers, clever enough to invent computers, jet planes, moon ships, antibiotics, and weapons of race suicide, are not wise enough to know their own sons, who are now shaping the values of America and will soon *be* America.

A quarter century ago next month, with V-J Day, the United States emerged from the war into modern times.

By JOHN BROOKS

5

In the subsequent twenty years, while the nation's adults, the prewar generation, were unwittingly removing from their own and their children's lives the physical underpinnings of the old national faiths and attitudes, they were also continuing—in fact, accelerating—the long process of social amelioration that had gone on, though not uninterruptedly, since not long after the Civil War. The first postwar quarter century was one of outstanding social as well as material progress.

About five years ago, I undertook a study of social change in the United States over the twenty-five years between the outbreak of the Second World War in 1939 and the mid-sixties. I found, among other things, that the great corporations, considered so gigantic and sinister in 1939, had become many times more gigantic and —in the pretty-well-substantiated public view—a good deal less sinister. (In the late thirties the Temporary National Economic Committee had reported with awe that General Motors, perhaps the archetypical American corporation, had assets of one billion dollars; less than two decades later General Motors would have *annual profits after taxes* of one billion dollars. It would meanwhile have abandoned its former rather surly attitude toward society and become a corporation as enlightened as most in its social attitudes.) The gross national product over the period had gone from 90 billion to 630 billion dollars a year; the federal budget had swollen from around nine billion to over one hundred billion; national income per capita had risen from nine hundred to well over three thousand dollars, while the national population (in sharp contradiction to the glum demographic predictions of 1939 that the nation faced a people shortage) had risen from 130,000,000 to over 190,000,000. Taxes and other forces had brought about a vast and generally beneficent redistribution of national wealth. Computer technology, in 1939 just a gleam in a few scientists' eyes, was already on the way to bringing about a new era in science and technology and, more obviously at first, in business methods; and the initial fears that computers would throw millions of people out of their jobs were beginning to prove unfounded. Poverty had by no means been eliminated, but by almost any fair-minded standard it had been sharply reduced; indeed, my calculations showed that by the standards applied in 1964, Franklin D. Roosevelt's one third of a nation ill fed, ill housed, and ill clothed in the thirties had been a gross understatement.

I found that over the period under study there had been a vast tidal migration from farms to cities. Thirty-one million Americans, or a quarter of the population, were farmers in 1939; only thirteen million, or less than 7 per cent, were still on the farms by 1964. The effect of this influx on the cities and on the new urbanites themselves, despite crime and overcrowding and suburbia

and urban sprawl, had not proved to be all bad. I found a tremendous rise in formal education: the average American was an elementary-school graduate in 1939, a high-school graduate by 1964; 15 per cent of college-age Americans attended college in 1939, well over 40 per cent in 1964.

Further, I argued that anti-Semitism, a strong and ominous thread in our national warp in 1939, had ceased

by 1964 to be an important factor—permanently, I patriotically supposed. On the question of Negro rights and privileges the evidence of progress, though more equivocal, was present. In 1964, in the nation's capital city, where in 1939 no black man had been suffered to eat in a public restaurant used by whites or to register in any hotel, Congress was passing a wide-ranging civil rights act, and the next year it would pass a far wider-ranging one. A long, painful campaign for civil rights in the South, beginning with the Supreme Court's first desegregation decision in 1954, had caught the national imagination and that of our Texan President himself, and as a result of increased black-voter registration Negroes were being elected to office at many levels in most parts of the country. Economically, to be sure, the average black man was only slightly better off in relation to the average white man than he had been in 1939. Formerly his income had been somewhat less than half of the white man's; now it was slightly more than half. But in 1964 the country seemed to have the will to tackle even this anomaly. One felt, buoyantly, that with the political liberation of the Negro virtually accomplished, his economic liberation was next on the agenda.

In its foreign affairs I said that the United States, which with the end of the war had assumed free-world leadership for the first time, had handled this generally unwanted responsibility fairly well in spite of some spectacular bungling. There were, despite moral arguments advanced in their behalf, such egregious disasters as the Bay of Pigs, the ill-starred U-2 reconnaissance flight, the unfortunate (but then not yet overwhelmingly tragic) miscalculation of our involvement in Vietnam. But there was also the nuclear test-ban treaty of 1963, the relief programs all over the world, and, of course, the Marshall Plan, which through its backers' statesmanlike vision of where enlightened self-interest lay, had done so much to set flattened Europe back on its feet.

In sum, my research convinced me that "the quarter-century . . . had seen such rapid and far-reaching changes in many aspects of American life as are not only unprecedented in our own national experience, but may well be unprecedented in that of any nation other than those that have been suddenly transformed by . . . war or plague." And I concluded that while the enormous material gains of the quarter century had unquestionably had their moral costs, the moral loss was far less clear than the material gain. America could not patly be said to have "sold its soul for mediocrity."

So I wrote then. Between then and now, over the past five years, many but not all of the trends I noted have continued. Economic growth has gone on to the point where most economists believe that 1971 will be the year when our gross national product will pass the all but inscrutable figure of a trillion dollars a year. Our 1964 federal budget is now almost doubled. Poverty, more and more in the news, is nevertheless still decreasing in fact.

On the other hand the migration from farms to cities has slowed sharply. Anti-Semitism in a new form has made an ominous appearance among Negro militants. Racial integration of schools has failed tragically, as shown by the fact that at the beginning of 1970—sixteen years after the Supreme Court's desegregation decision—less than one fifth of southern Negro pupils and hardly more than one fourth of northern and western Negro pupils were attending predominantly white

schools. The stagnation of black economic status is shown by the persistence of two familiar statistics—black income still just over half that of whites, black unemployment still double that among whites.

But statistics are not all. There exist also national moods, and they rather than statistics reflect attitudes and values. There are fashions in statistics; appropriate ones can be found to fit any mood, to buttress any conventional wisdom, and it can be argued that the moods give birth to the figures rather than vice versa. At any rate, some time recently, probably in 1965, the national mood reversed itself as dramatically as a manic-depressive patient goes from the heights to the depths, and I see my study as having been completed in the last, climactic days of a period of national euphoria.

The trigger for the mood change is harder to identify. Many would equate it with the hateful trigger of Lee Harvey Oswald's mail-order gun in Dallas in November, 1963, and contend that the accomplishments of 1964 and early 1965 were the result of accumulated momentum—that, indeed, the productive phase of the Kennedy administration was actually the year and a half after John Kennedy's death. Others would choose the Watts riots of August, 1965, the first time the murderous and suicidal rage and despair of urban blacks outside the South was revealed; perhaps the largest number would choose the escalation of the Vietnam war, which began with the bombing of North Vietnam that February. At all events the change occurred, and the nation went into the valley of a shadow from which it has not yet emerged as this is written.

In terms of inner change, of change in American attitudes and American values, these last five years have surely been the crucial ones in the quarter century since V-J Day. And these changes, which I propose to examine here as cheerfully as possible, seem of such a magnitude that every American except the very young, the very empty, and the very enclosed must now, to some extent, feel himself a foreigner in his native land.

Better than statistics, as a starting point for a study of moods, are words. The 1947 *Britannica Book of the Year* gave a list of words that, according to its authorities, "became prominent or were seemingly used for the first time" in either 1945 or 1946. Predictably enough, some of the listed words were of only ephemeral usefulness and have vanished without leaving a trace; for example, *athodyd* (a ramjet engine), *cuddle seat* (a contrivance for carrying small children, both word and device introduced by Australian war brides), and *Huff-Duff* (a navigation aid for ships and planes that was quickly superseded). But a surprising number of the new coinages survive,

CONTINUED ON PAGE 68

F.D.R.
THE LAST JOURNEY

By JAMES MacGREGOR BURNS

When Franklin Delano Roosevelt was inaugurated for the fourth time, in January, 1945, twelve years of guiding the country through depression and war had sapped the strength of this vital and complex man. His health, which had been a major issue in the 1944 campaign, was the constant concern of his dedicated staff. Roosevelt himself, by this time, was thinking mostly of the problems of the coming peace. The following article is excerpted from James MacGregor Burns's Roosevelt: The Soldier of Freedom, *which will be published in September by Harcourt, Brace & World. This book, which follows the author's earlier biography,* Roosevelt: The Lion and the Fox, *completes Mr. Burns's distinguished and engrossing study of the thirty-second President of the United States. Several sentences from the earlier book are included in this excerpt. Among his sources, the author is especially indebted to Bernard Asbell's* When F. D. R. Died.

If events abroad were reaching one of the great climacterics of history, domestic affairs by the spring of 1945 were following their own tepid cycle. In the wake of the President's State of the Union messages in January, the committees of Congress assumed command of the legislative process with their ancient weapons of discussion, dilution, and delay. The manpower bill, after passing the House, slowly bled to death in the Senate as victories abroad blunted the spur of emergency. Former Vice President Henry Wallace was finally confirmed as Secretary of Commerce, replacing Jesse Jones. The confirmation came only after a bitter struggle in the Senate —and only after the big federal lending agencies were separated from Commerce so that Wallace could not "control" billions in loans. Congressional investigators of subversive activities conducted feckless witch hunts.

Not for years had the President's legislative fortunes seemed at such a low ebb. The Republican and Democratic congressional parties were collaborating smoothly. Roosevelt, however, seemed hardly aware of the congressional situation; in any event he was not going to invite a quarrel with the legislators over domestic matters when he needed Republican and conservative support for his foreign policies, especially for American leadership in the planned new international organization.

His administration ran on with the momentum of twelve years of liberal activism. He urged renewal and strengthening of the Trade Agreements Act. He asked for an inquiry into guaranteed annual wage plans. He received ambassadors, awarded medals, discussed jobs with Democratic politicos.

He seemed to be dwelling in the past and the future, as well as the present. "I still say, thank God for those good old days and for old and tried friends like you,"

"It was a processional of terrible simplicity and a march too solemn for tears"

he wrote to a Dutchess County friend who had remarked that it was a long step from the size of apple barrels—an issue in Roosevelt's 1912 campaign—to meeting Churchill and Stalin and perhaps deciding the fate of the world. He was looking forward to his trips to San Francisco in April to the conference scheduled for organizing the United Nations and to England later in the spring with his wife. And by late March he could relax about military prospects in Europe. When he told Frances Perkins of his projected trip to England and she protested that it was still too dangerous, he put his hand to the side of his mouth and whispered: "The war in Europe will be over by the end of May."

Both his daughter, Anna Boettiger, and his devoted secretary, Grace Tully, were quietly trying to conserve the President's strength until he could get some rest at Warm Springs. Both were perplexed by sudden changes in his appearance. So were the reporters, who were watching him closely. At the White House correspondents' dinner Allen Drury, correspondent for the United Press, noted how old and thin and scrawny-necked he looked when he was wheeled in, how he stared out at the crowded tables as though he did not see the people, how he failed to respond to the blare of trumpets and to the applause.

Then he suddenly came to life, Drury noted, and began to enjoy himself. The notables of Washington were there, including Admiral Leahy and General Marshall, Cabinet members Byrnes and Ickes and Biddle and Morgenthau, Supreme Court Justices Douglas and Jackson, several important senators, and Vice President Truman, with a handkerchief carefully folded in his breast pocket so that the four corners showed. Danny Kaye performed, and Jimmy Durante and Fanny Brice. Everyone watched the greatest performer of all—how he steadily drank wine and smoked his uplifted cigarette, how he leaned forward with his hand cupped behind his ear to hear a joke repeated as laughter welled up in the room, how his booming laughter rang out. Then a few moments later observers noticed how he simply sat at the table

In this picture taken at Saki Airport in Yalta in February, 1945, Roosevelt looked prophetically gaunt and ill as compared with the chubby-faced Churchill and the rugged-looking Molotov at the left.

with an intent, vague expression on his face, while his jaw dropped and his mouth fell open.

But he lasted out the evening and gave a talk at the end. He would speak about humanity, he said—"We all love humanity, you love humanity, I love humanity. . . ." And in the name of humanity he would give them a headline story—"I am calling off the press conference for tomorrow morning."

The applause rang out as he was shifted back to his wheel chair, Drury noted in his diary, "and just before he went out the door he acknowledged it with the old, familiar gesture, so that the last we saw of Franklin Roosevelt was the head going up with a toss, the smile breaking out, the hand uplifted and waving in the old, familiar way."

The usual crowd clustered around the little Warm Springs station as Roosevelt's train pulled in on Good Friday, March 30, 1945. Something seemed different this time as Roosevelt's big frame, slumped in the wheel chair, seemed to joggle uncontrollably as he was rolled along the platform. A murmur drifted through the crowd. But the President drove his own car to the Little White House on top of the hill.

That evening William Hassett, a presidential secretary, told Dr. Howard G. Bruenn that the President was slipping away. Hassett blurted out that he had been maintaining a bluff to the family and even to Roosevelt himself, but he felt there was no hope for him. His signature had become feeble—the bold stroke and heavy line of old were gone, or simply faded out. Dr. Bruenn cautiously granted that Roosevelt was in a precarious condition but said it was not hopeless if he could be protected from emotional and mental strain. That was impossible, Hassett said. He and Bruenn were on the verge of despair.

But after a few days in the warm Georgia sun Roose-

*"how old and thin he looked
when he was wheeled in, how he stared
as though he did not see the people"*

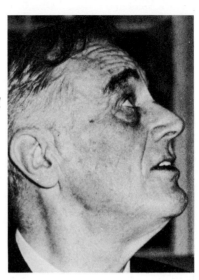

velt's gray pallor changed and some of his old vitality returned, though his blood pressure had become erratic, ranging between 170/88 and 240/130. The news from Europe was exciting: American, British, and Canadian troops were encircling the Ruhr, spearing northwest toward Hanover and Bremen, driving ever deeper into the heart of Germany. Reports were also coming to Washington of the many thousands of civilian deaths in the fire bombings of Japanese and German cities; it is doubtful that Roosevelt understood the enormity of the civilian losses, which would compare with the effects of the later atomic bombings.

Stalin's harsh messages were forwarded to Warm Springs. Roosevelt was disturbed but not depressed by his deteriorating relations with the Kremlin. Unlike Churchill, who at the time foresaw the darkness ahead, as he said later, and moved amid cheering crowds with an aching heart, Roosevelt was sure that things would be put right. He tried to calm the troubled waters, cabling Stalin that in any event there must not be mutual distrust. He urged on Churchill that the Soviet problem be minimized as much as possible; things would straighten out. He added: "We must be firm however, and our course thus far is correct."

The President seemed more concerned with Asia than with Europe during these early April days. He was pleased with the news of the sudden fall of the Japanese cabinet in the wake of the invasion of Okinawa. Philippine President Sergio Osmeña was back in the United States to report on the terrible destruction in Manila. The President talked with reporters in remarkable detail about conditions in the Philippines, economic problems, the need for American assistance. It was his 998th press conference.

He was especially determined that there be no change in plans for immediate independence for the Philippines. It depended only on how quickly the Japanese were cleared from the islands. He would set an example for the British and the other colonial powers. He wrote to

his old Navy Department chief, Josephus Daniels, that he would like independence to go into effect in August and to be present himself, but he feared he might have to be in Europe for a conference about that time.

On the afternoon of April 11 the President dictated the draft of a speech for Jefferson Day: "Americans are gathered together in communities all over the country to pay tribute to the living memory of Thomas Jefferson —one of the greatest of all democrats; and I want to make it clear that I am spelling that word 'democrats' with a small *d*. . . ."

The President paid tribute to Jefferson as Secretary of State, President, and scientist. Then he continued:

The once powerful, malignant Nazi state is crumbling. The Japanese war lords are receiving, in their own homeland, the retribution for which they asked when they attacked Pearl Harbor.

But the mere conquest of our enemies is not enough.

We must go on to do all in our power to conquer the doubts and the fears, the ignorance and the greed, which made this horror possible. . . .

Today we are faced with the pre-eminent fact that, if civilization is to survive, we must cultivate the science of human relationships—the ability of all peoples, of all kinds, to live together and work together, in the same world, at peace.

Let me assure you that my hand is the steadier for the work that is to be done, that I move more firmly into the task, knowing that you—millions and millions of you—are joined with me in the resolve to make this work endure.

The work, my friends, is peace. More than an end of this war—an end to the beginnings of all wars. Yes, an end, forever, to this impractical, unrealistic settlement of the differences between governments by the mass killing of peoples.

Today, as we move against the terrible scourge of war—as we go forward toward the greatest contribution that any generation of human beings can make in this world—the contribution of lasting peace, I ask you to keep up your faith. I measure the sound, solid achievement that can be made at this time by the straight edge of your own confidence and your resolve. And to you, and to all Americans who dedicate themselves with us to the making of an abiding peace, I say: The only limit

CONTINUED ON PAGE 78

11

Some years before Nicholas Trist went to Mexico on his thorny mission at the age of forty-seven, Charles Bird King painted this portrait of him. Opposite: A device from a Mexican battle flag captured by American troops

THE THANKLESS TASK OF
NICHOLAS TRIST

*You are conducting secret peace talks with the enemy in the
midst of an unpopular and interminable foreign war. The American field
commander is throwing every obstacle in your path.
Then, just as the talks are getting somewhere, the President orders you home.
What do you do now?*

As winter wore on into the spring of 1847, the hope grew in Washington that the year-old war with Mexico might be settled soon. The nation's first major foreign conflict had been an unpopular affair from the beginning; a large number of Americans seem to have thought it would be a short skirmish, followed by a rich land-grab, and were disappointed when the Mexicans showed no immediate signs of collapsing or negotiating. When President James K. Polk learned of General Winfield Scott's victory on March 27 at Veracruz, he concluded that the moment was auspicious for peace talks and, with the agreement of his Cabinet, looked about for a man he might send to Scott's headquarters to be on the scene should the Mexicans decide to sue for peace.

A Democrat who had already decided not to seek re-election in 1848, the President was eager for the war to end, but he had no intention of appointing someone who would make political hay out of an important peace mission. He realized he had to select someone "who would be satisfactory to the country . . . [yet] such is the jealousy of the different factions of the Democratic party in reference to the next Presidential Election toward each other that it is impossible to appoint any prominent man." And so it was that Nicholas Philip Trist

was chosen for one of the strangest, most misunderstood, most productive assignments in American diplomatic history.

At the time Polk plucked him out of near-anonymity for greater things, Trist was the chief clerk in the State Department. This meant that he was second-in-command to the Secretary, James Buchanan—a position he had attained largely through his intimate connections with some of the towering figures in United States politics. Trist had been born in 1800 in Charlottesville, Virginia, where his grandmother was a close friend of Thomas Jefferson, and as a result of that relationship Nicholas and his brothers were invited to come to Monticello for an extended visit in 1817. There Nicholas promptly fell in love with Mr. Jefferson's granddaughter Virginia Jefferson Randolph (a tall girl of "not great personal charms," as Trist's outspoken mother described her) and asked permission to marry her. Virginia's mother and Nicholas' found this prospect chilling, since he was only eighteen and she seventeen; September and young Trist's departure for the Military Academy at West Point came none too soon to suit either of them. At the academy the new cadet showed certain traits that remained with him all his life: he hated restrictions and discipline; he was frequently ill (with his frail constitution—

By RICHARD M. KETCHUM

he was 6 feet tall and weighed only 120 pounds—he had difficulty throwing off colds); he worried incessantly; he wrote interminable letters to his family and friends; and he persisted in a belief that Virginians were a very special people, superior to the inhabitants of other parts of the country. At West Point he became a close friend of young Andrew Jackson Donelson, nephew of the hero of New Orleans—an association that was to have an important effect on his later career.

In the summer of 1821 Trist returned to Monticello, determined to quit West Point, marry Virginia Randolph, and take up the law. This time he was granted permission to propose to his inamorata but lost his nerve at the crucial moment and instead wrote her a letter the next day: "The interview of yesterday," he admitted, "was for the purpose of making a declaration of a passion that you must have often read in me." But once again he was rebuffed, this time by the girl herself, who did not want to leave her family just then and suggested that Trist return to Louisiana—where he had grown up—and read law there. He followed her advice, and three years later he was back at Monticello, where they were married at last on September 11, 1824.

Trist continued his study of the law with Thomas Jefferson and became the feeble ex-President's part-time secretary, riding and walking companion, and confidant. In long talks together Jefferson spoke to him about his views on all the events and personalities of the day, and the old man and the young one developed a truly close friendship. When the Trists' first child was born in May, 1826, she was named for Jefferson's wife; the baby was Jefferson's first great-grandchild and the only one he lived to see, for by this time he was confined to bed most of the time. Trist was with him almost constantly, writing his last letters and conversing for hours with the man who had befriended him. The old statesman was determined to live until July 4, the fiftieth anniversary of the Declaration of Independence he had written, and his last weeks were a triumph of will. All through the night of July 3 Trist remained at his side; with an effort Jefferson asked if it were midnight yet, and when Trist replied that it was, the dying man smiled and murmured, "Ah, just as I wished." A few hours later he was dead.

To Trist, as an administrator of Jefferson's estate, fell the chief burden of settling the former President's chaotic financial affairs (less than five thousand dollars remained in his bank account when he died, and the estate was sorely pressed for funds to run Monticello and support the large family that continued to live there). But despite the demands made upon him, Trist completed his law studies and in November, 1826, was admitted to the Virginia bar. Then followed a brief and unsuccessful ownership of a newspaper, until Trist received an offer of a clerkship in the Department of State from the Secretary,

Henry Clay. The job paid fourteen hundred dollars a year, and he accepted with pleasure. Luckily, when Andrew Jackson became President in 1829, Trist's friendship with Jefferson, Madison, and Jackson's nephew Donelson was remembered; unlike so many victims of the spoils system, he was allowed to stay on in his job. Soon Trist and his wife became regulars at White House dinners; Jackson was especially interested in hearing from them about Jefferson's political beliefs, his views on emancipation of the slaves, and his ideas concerning religious freedom.

At the Jefferson memorial birthday dinner in 1830 Trist gave what was technically the chief toast—to the memory of the late President—but his remarks were considerably overshadowed by those of Andrew Jackson: this was the famous occasion on which Jackson rose to his feet, fixed would-be secessionist John C. Calhoun with a steely eye, and stated unequivocally, "Our Union: It must be preserved."

At this time Trist's fluent knowledge of Spanish made him one of the principal State Department informants on Latin-American countries; he was also beginning to handle most of the correspondence between the United States and Russia while James Buchanan was minister there. And opportunity knocked, oddly enough, as a result of a grand social brouhaha at the White House. By spring of 1830 the members of Jackson's Cabinet had taken sides over Peggy O'Neale Eaton, a former barmaid who had become the second wife of John Eaton, the Secretary of War, and while the President stubbornly supported her, the Cabinet officers (except Secretary of State Martin Van Buren) and their wives would have nothing to do with her. Mrs. Andrew Jackson Donelson withdrew as the President's hostess rather than call on her, and suddenly Trist was asked to assume Donelson's place as Jackson's private secretary.

Diplomats, congressmen, and Cabinet officers transacted business through him; it was a demanding, time-consuming position of great responsibility and long hours, from which Trist—fortunately for his relations with his family—was relieved in 1831 by Donelson's reconciliation with his uncle. Then, after two more years in the State Department, Trist received a presidential appointment that promised an opportunity to do something on his own. By now a man of polished manners, impeccable connections, keen insight, and with a broad grounding in foreign affairs, he became consul at the Cuban port of Havana.

He had not been in Havana long before he realized that it had been a mistake to come; it was not a good post for anyone with ambition. The tedious tropical hours found Trist writing incredibly long letters and reports to Washington—reports so full of trivia one wonders if the recipients ever finished reading them (one communication to the Senate Committee on Finance contained fifty-two closely written pages). This was, however, one of the few times in his life that Trist made anything like enough money; he seems to have picked up substantial sums outside his job through notary fees and by investing funds that were deposited with him. But in 1839 some ugly charges were made against Trist—accusations of inefficiency, failure to support American interests, and abetting the slave trade—and his conduct was reviewed by a congressional committee. Although the congressmen gave him a clean bill of health, Trist seems to have been negligent, at the very least, and perhaps even guilty of some of the charges made against him. Certainly many U.S. captains who touched at Havana were highly critical of the consul and his activities. In any case, merit—or the lack of it—sometimes counted for less than the spoils system, and in 1841 Trist received word from the new Whig Secretary of State, Daniel Webster, that he was relieved of his consular duties. Four years later the political tides changed once more, James K. Polk became President, Trist's old friend James Buchanan was appointed Secretary of State, and Trist was named chief clerk of the department. The dying Andrew Jackson, ever a man to support a friend, wrote to Polk endorsing Trist for the job, which paid two thousand dollars a year.

And so it came about, early in 1847, that President Polk decided to send Nicholas P. Trist as his emissary to Mexico, there to await the proper moment to enter into negotiations with a shaky Mexican government. Despite his disappointing performance in Cuba, Trist seemed a natural for the post: in addition to his fluency in Spanish he was thoroughly knowledgeable about the workings of the State Department; as a loyal Democrat he was known to Polk and to members of the Cabinet, yet he had never been active in politics and appeared to have no ambitions in that direction. His assignment, quite simply, was to make his way as inconspicuously as possible to General Winfield Scott's headquarters in Mexico and to forward to the enemy government, via the American commanding general, a proposed treaty of peace drafted by the Secretary of State and approved by administration leaders in Washington. If, by the time he arrived there, the Mexicans had already designated a plenipotentiary empowered to conclude a treaty, Trist was to begin negotiations with him on the basis of the American draft. Its terms were quite definite and had been

President James K. Polk as he looked in 1846, shortly before Trist engineered the acquisition of territory that was to become Polk's chief claim to fame. In recompense, Polk fired Trist.

BY THOMAS CASILEAR COLE AFTER G. P. A. HEALY; U.S. NAVAL ACADEMY MUSEUM

drawn by Polk and Buchanan in the uneasy awareness that the congressional opposition was ready to pounce on the slightest misstep as a means of repudiating the administration on "the Mexican question." This draft treaty had been submitted to the Cabinet on April 13; revised and approved by both President and Cabinet, it was delivered on April 15, 1847, to Nicholas P. Trist, who was designated a "commissioner plenipotentiary" and bidden Godspeed.

Secrecy, of course, was absolutely vital to the mission, and Polk had every confidence in the discretion of his emissary; but Trist had been gone less than a week when reports of his assignment appeared in the New York *Herald*, the *National Intelligencer*, *Niles' Weekly Register*, and other newspapers. Polk was understandably furious and alternated between blaming Trist and the State Department for the unpardonable leak (finally he settled on the latter as the most likely source and took a dislike to Buchanan that hardened as time wore on). From New Orleans the unsuspecting Trist wrote one of his wearisome letters to his chief; in thirty verbose pages the only real news he gave Buchanan was that he had arrived in Louisiana after travelling overland via Charleston, Augusta, and Mobile, whence he had taken a steamer to New Orleans. Travelling incognito as "Doctor Tarreau," a French merchant, he had stayed at a "French auberge, of the economical order," rather than at one of the better hotels where someone might recognize him and become suspicious.

For all his precautions Trist managed to call a good deal of attention to himself by his painstaking selection of a vessel to carry him quickly toward his destination; from New Orleans he sailed across the Gulf of Mexico in eight days, arriving on May 6 at Veracruz, where he learned that a supply train would leave on the eighth for Scott's headquarters. And here Trist made a monumental error.

He bore with him a letter of appointment from Buchanan, giving him "full diplomatic powers" to sign a treaty in the name of the United States. He also had two copies of the treaty *projet*, or draft—one of them sealed, for the Mexicans—and his instructions were to place the sealed copy in the hands of General Scott for forwarding to the Mexican authorities. But unfortunately, instead of delivering this document to Scott personally and inform-

CONTINUED ON PAGE 86

"Rebels, turn

In the chill darkness of an October night in 1781 six young American seamen—unaware that the tide of war was shifting dramatically to the side of the colonists—pried the iron bars off a starboard port on a grim hulk anchored in the East River. Close by on the larboard side lay the rural shore of Brooklyn—a sparsely settled area with only the Remsen farmhouse and barn visible from the ship. In the distance off the ship's starboard was the northernmost end of the port town of New York, occupied like Long Island by the British since the war's beginning. One by one the sailors lowered themselves on a rope held by shipmates, dropped quietly into the dark water, and swam aft to huddle beneath the stern until the marine guard on the deck turned on his rounds and paced forward. Then they struck off for a point on the Long Island shore some two miles distant, beyond the British sentries.

The last to leave, a young boy who was a poor swimmer, panicked as he saw his companions pull away from him. "Oh! lord have mercy, I shall be drowned!" he shouted. Officers of the night watch on the quarter-deck heard him and launched a boat after the escapees. The terror-stricken youth grabbed the gunwale, only to have one of his hands whacked so hard "that the bone was laid bare." He was then bayoneted by the guard, hauled aboard, and taken back to the ship, where he died of his wounds the next day. Four of his friends, though stronger swimmers, were shot and killed in the water. The sixth man, who lived to tell the story, circled back to the bow and clung to the anchor chain, with only his nose protruding from the water, until the guards gave up their search. When dawn broke and the upper deck of the old hulk was again swarming with life, the chilled and exhausted survivor climbed up the chain and escaped detection by disappearing into the shaggy mass of humanity.

The fate from which the six made their ill-destined attempt to escape—a fate more dreaded than the lethal penalty of failure—was detention aboard the British prison ship *Jersey*. She was the most notorious of a dozen decrepit prison and hospital ships moored by the British in a bay in the East River that would later be the site of the Brooklyn Navy Yard. A retired man-of-war, *Jersey* had once carried sixty-four guns and a crew of four hundred officers and men during nearly forty years of undistinguished service in the Mediterranean and Caribbean. When the American Revolution began, she had been idle six years, disarmed and used as a hospital ship in England. In May, 1776, she sailed in a fleet of transports carrying Hessian mercenaries to the colonies. After three years in New York harbor as successively a floating

By ARTHUR B. TOURTELLOT

A nineteenth-century painting caught something of the aura of menace that enveloped Jersey*'s hulk like an invisible shroud.*

storehouse and a hospital ship, she became a prison ship in 1780. During the next three and a half years an estimated eleven thousand American seamen died on her rotting decks.

British men-of-war were majestic, handsome vessels: three towering masts carrying billowing square sails and topped with bright pennants; gaily painted and extravagantly decorated sterns; bright and imaginatively carved figureheads; and great, solid hulls that could withstand the pounding of the high seas and still move with massive grace in sheltered waters. But as a prison ship, *Jersey* was a gloomy, depressing sight. Her masts, rigging, and all her spars save the bowsprit were gone. A gaunt, gallowslike hoist to lift supplies aboard was her only superstructure. Her elaborate figurehead, a rampant royal lion, had been taken away for use on an active vessel. Rudderless, she rested on her keel at low tide on the oozy bottom of the bay. Ebenezer Fox, a sixteen-year-old cabin steward aboard the Massachusetts frigate *Protector*, captured by the British off Sandy Hook, was plunged into despair by the very sight of *Jersey*, as a sloop carried him and his shipmates up the river to their imprisonment. "The portholes were closed and secured," he later wrote. "Two tiers of holes were cut through her sides, about two feet square and about ten feet apart, strongly guarded by a grating of iron bars. . . . The idea of being a prisoner in such a place was sufficient to fill the mind with grief and distress. The heart sickened. . . ."

Thomas Dring, veteran of another prison ship, named with bitter irony *Good Hope*, remembered something more pungent about his initial contact with the ship. As the boat neared the accommodation ladder that led to the gangway on *Jersey*'s larboard side, ". . . my station in the boat, as she hauled alongside, was exactly opposite to one of the air-ports in the side of the ship. From this aperture, proceeded a strong current of foul vapour, of a kind to which I had been before accustomed, while confined on board the *Good Hope;* the peculiarly disgusting smell of which, I then recollected, after a lapse of three years. This was, however, far more foul and loathsome than any thing which I had ever met with on board that ship, and produced a sensation of nausea far beyond my powers of description."

Once they were aboard, neither the stark surroundings nor the routine and deprivations to which they were subjected gave Fox, Dring, and their fellow prisoners any reassurance. Nor were they meant to do so. Although the weapons of war in the eighteenth century were less devastating than those of today, life at sea was raw, cruel, and violent—in war and in peacetime. Beat-

CONTINUED ON PAGE 90

GRAVEN IMAGES
Sermons in Stones

Footnoting the history of our Puritan ancestors are the legends left on stone among the countless burying grounds of early New England. These gravestones with their poignant inscriptions and symbolic imagery possess an eloquence rarely matched in the annals of colonial literature. They speak directly to all who confront them, echoing the past and reminding us of the incredible hardships endured by those early pioneers. On their crumbling surfaces one can trace the history of our nation—its wars and epidemics; its religious and political attitudes; its changing fashions in art and rhetoric; and, above all, the moving accounts of personal tragedy that tried the souls of its people.

There is a great wealth of art and design in colonial burying grounds. One may still see on the weathered sandstone, slate, and marble slabs crowding close beside old meeting houses or standing aslant on desolate, wind-swept hills, the symbolic carvings that constitute our largest body of early American stone sculpture. It was here that the sacred and secular sentiments of our forefathers found expression at the hands of native stone-cutters; they managed in the confines of their rigid society to convey an astonishing diversity of pictorial images, not only reflecting the attitudes of their time but also reaching beyond them in vision and originality.

These masters of mallet and chisel decorated their stones with winged death's-heads and a variety of angels. They carved birds, flowers, and intricate geometric patterns. They tried their hands at portraiture. They imagined the fruits of the Kingdom of Heaven and recreated them in stone. They carved suns, skeletons, hourglasses, scythes, and all manner of symbolic objects. They inscribed their stones with enduring epitaphs that still measure the thoughts of a people, in bold, serviceable lettering that ranged from the crudest to the most highly sophisticated calligraphy. And then, incredibly, within a few short years, while at the height of their creative powers, they switched to a standardized urn-and-willow-tree design and gave themselves over to its dull and endless repetition.

Cemetery browsing is particularly rewarding in New England, where generations of imaginative stone carvers have left a rich legacy of source material for historians, sociologists, genealogists, medical researchers, folk-lorists, and any number of people seeking clues to our past. A diligent student can trace movements of immigrating settlers or compile a catalogue of the strange and fascinating names imposed upon their progeny. Artists can derive pleasure and new inspiration from old designs. The calligrapher can find alphabets beyond his wildest dreams.

The early colonists generally followed English custom by placing their common burying grounds adjacent to their meeting houses, in full, ominous view of the worshippers. As the eighteenth century progressed, gravestones of influential men—deacons, doctors, merchants, sea captains, military figures, people of means and those who had earned the respect of their communities—became taller and more ornate. The best of them featured wordy inscriptions with whole histories carved in verse to complement the iconography that stood as the individual stonecutter's stock in trade. There was a certain confirmation of status in having one's good deeds and personal attributes recorded on stone for all to see and remember. A good example, with typically free style, appears on a stone in Farmington, Connecticut:

Here Lieth Interr'd the Body of
Mr NOAH ANDRUSS: Graduated
at yale College, A.D. 1777, & Departed
this life of ℣ 29th of May; 1780: a

18   *Gravestone Rubbings by* AVON NEAL *and* ANN PARKER
Text by AVON NEAL

Sacred to the Memory
of Amasa Brainard Jr
Son of Lieut Amasa & Mrs
Jedidah Brainard who
receiv'd a Mortal wound on his head
by the falling of a weight from the Bell
on Sunday ye 22nd of Apl 1798
as he was about to enter the Church
to attend on divine worship
who Departed this life
April 27th in ye 20 in Year of
his Age

The rubbing above is taken from the top of a stone in Hingham, Massachusetts, dated 1783, which declares: "Here lies the Remains of Capt. Samuel Linclon [sic] and his two wives, Fanna and Mary." A glance at the three stony countenances is assurance enough that all was prim and proper. The monument at right surmounts all that is mortal of the Reverend Silas Biglow, who was buried at Paxton, Massachusetts, in 1769. Like the faces on these pages, the figure presents man in a stylized form, and not in any likeness. The minister stands before a lectern adorned with tassels, the Good Book in his hand. The flanking Tuscan columns indicate the growing influence of Georgian themes upon mortuary sculpture. Winged heads of angels celebrate either the world to come or the flight of the soul to immortality.

20

This angel adorns the gravestone of
Polly Coombes, whose soul took wing
at Bellingham, Mass., in 1795. The
depiction, which has an unusually
genial if not a positively frolicsome
look, is (alas) Polly's soul, not Polly.

At right is a rare example of an angel in full figure, carved on the tomb of Charles Stuart, who died at Peterboro, New Hampshire, in 1802. The angel seems to float beneath the overhanging, tassled top of the tomb, while the trumpet is an emblem of Judgment Day, when our ancestors knew that the dead would be summoned forth again from the grave.

In a wooded burying ground at Grafton, Vermont, stands the curious grave of Rebecca Park and her fourteen infants. The material of their memorial is gray slate, and the artist used a compass to draw the tiny faces, arranging thirteen of them in a circular pattern as blossoms on a tree of eternal life. Why the fourteenth has a separate place at center, we cannot say, but the result is one of the most singularly artistic stones to be found in all of New England.

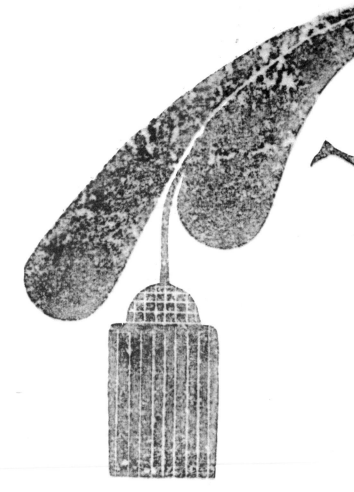

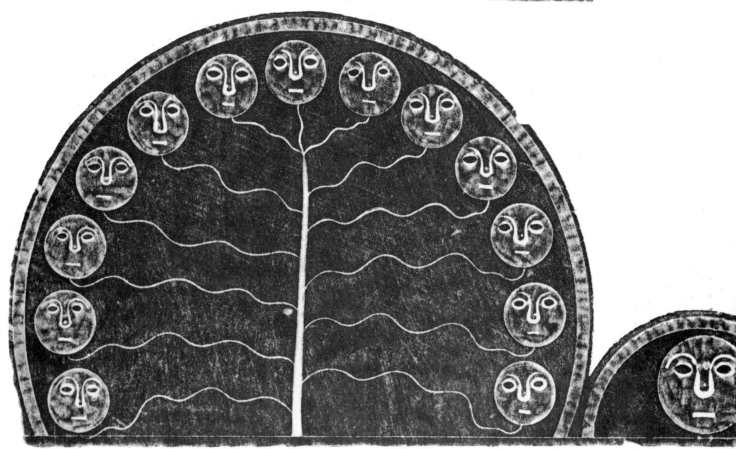

The stone below, shown in its entirety, includes many of the more picturesque symbols—an angel, a skeleton (mortality), the Reaper, the hourglass (hora fugit). Stone lettering like this may serve to remind us that "ye" is only an abbreviation for "the," was pronounced "the," and merely provided our forefathers a space-saver. Why are two years of death shown? Before English calendar reform in 1752, the Old Style year was eleven days behind the Continental year and was reckoned as beginning March 25. This date, Jan. 6, 1698, Old Style, is Jan. 17, 1699, New.

SANCTORUM MEMORIA SIT BEATA

HERE LYETH BURIED
Yᵉ BODY OF
Mᴿ TIMOHY LINDALL
AGED 56 YEARS
& 7 Mᵒ DECEASE
JANUARY Yᵉ 6
1 6 9 8/9

Above is a pathetic detail taken from the gravestone of Mary Harvey, of Deerfield, who was buried in 1785 with her infant in her arms. Coffins usually appear closed.

The gravestone above, of Colonel David Payson, who died at Wiscasset, Maine, in 1814, exhibits the eye of God, an arrow (God's instrument), and the trumpet at whose sound the dead should "be raised incorruptible." A vandal has added graffiti which endow the angel with female characteristics. Below: the death of John Stockbridge, of Hanover, Massachusetts, in 1768 is vividly recorded. He was laid low by a tree which he was chopping down, and the fatal axe is represented lying beside him.

young gentleman of good geniues, an
accomplished Scholar, evangelical prea
chur, amiable friend, & exhibited a bright
example of ẏ virtues, & graces of ẏ Chri
stian character.

Amidst continual references to noble qualities—words such as *virtuous, charitable, dutiful*—it is almost a relief to detect a discernible trend toward ostentatiousness among the members of this otherwise austere society. Even during their most trying times our ancestors could put aside their bereavement long enough to labor at outdoing a neighbor.

Gravestone verses reflected the feelings of the times—dire warnings to the living, Biblical quotations, and later, sentimental renderings extolling the virtues of the person entombed. One of the most common verses in use during colonial times was some variation of the familiar, "As you are now, so once was I," which had appeared in England as early as 1376 on the tomb of Edward, the Black Prince. It was paraphrased throughout New England, a typical version being:

> *Behold and see as you pass by*
> *As you are now, so once was I;*
> *As I am now, so you will be—*
> *Prepare for Death and follow me.*

During the Victorian era it was a popular pastime to stroll among the rows of lichen-covered stones deciphering epitaphs and copying off choice selections. Such collections were sometimes published in small editions for distribution among one's friends and relatives, thereby preserving much that has since been lost through neglect and vandalism. Epitaphs of the famous were most sought after, but it was the rare anthology that did not include at least one account of someone's strange or sudden demise, like that of Amasa Brainard, Jr., shown in our rubbing on page 19.

Much of the humor traditionally associated with New England cemeteries was unintentional. Since spelling had not yet been standardized, many unschooled stonecutters figured out their words phonetically. But these flawed messages, in spite of inconsistencies even in their misspellings, were usually direct and clear enough to those who first read them. It was not until later that aspiring sophisticates began to look upon such epitaphs as quaint. The gravestone for Marcy Halle in Glastonbury, Connecticut, who "decesed August the 21th, 1719, Aged 38 Years," epitomized this comedy of errors with a tortured bit of verse:

> *Here Lies one who*
> *os lifes thrads*
> *Cut a sunder She*
> *was strucke dead*
> *by a clap of thundr*

On a gravestone in Holyoke, Massachusetts, one can read that

> Mr. Nathl Parks
> Who on 21st of March 1794
> being out a hunting &
> Concealed in a ditch was
> Casually shot by
> Mr. Luther Frink

This was not, as a modern reader might think, a deliberate act of callousness. In modern times the word *casual* has come generally to mean "unconcerned," "offhand," or "careless," but its common meaning in those days was "accidental" or "unexpected."

A rather famous stone is that of Lieutenant Mehuman Hinsdell of Deerfield, Massachusetts, who died in 1736. Part of its text reads:

> . . . first male child born in this place and
> was twice captivated by the Indian salvages.

Salvage for *savage* appears in the *Oxford English Dictionary* as archaic, *captivate* for *capture* as obsolete. And the laughter thus dies down.

"My glass is run" was an expression quite common in the days when time was reckoned by hourglasses, and a life's brief span ended in the allegorical sense much as the sands in a glass were run. On at least two gravestones, those of James Ewins, 1781, of East Derry, New Hampshire, and Ebenezer Tinney, 1813, in Grafton, Vermont, an additional curvilinear cut extended the *n* to an *m* and therefore radically changed the implication.

One startling inscription included in many collections is, "Lord, she is thin." One can only speculate why the final *e* was dropped—forgetfulness, lack of space, or an attempted phonetic spelling; perhaps it was merely truth.

Epitaphs were often blunt in their accusations, and a visitor to an old cemetery might not be surprised to read that someone had been "Killed by unskilled Dr." or a woman was "Talked to death by friends." (It still happens.) Confirmed bachelors in Plymouth, Massachusetts, may well have thought that James Jordan, who "Drowned in Smelt Pond," had been spared a fate worse than death when he was "Buried on the day he was to have been Married." A stone in Providence, Rhode Island, tells a similar story:

> Sidney Snyder, 1823
> age 20
> *The wedding day*
> *decided was*
> *The wedding wine*
> *provided;*
> *But ere the day did*
> *come along*

He'd drunk it up and
died, did.
Ah Sidney! Ah Sidney!

In Bradford, Massachusetts, a monument was erected to the memory of Nathaniel Thurston, who finally met his match in 1811, aged fifty-six. In a row beside him stand six slate stones commemorating six of his seven wives.

According to a stone in New Haven, Connecticut, things were less harmonious for some husbands than others:

> Here lies the body of Obadiah Wilkinson
> And Ruth, his wife
> "Their warfare is accomplished"

Somehow, as could be expected, women continued to have the last word, even in death. In Burlington, Vermont, one learns:

> She lived with her husband fifty years
> And died in a confident hope of a better life.

Still another relict composed this possibly ambiguous tribute:

> *Stranger, call this not a place of*
> *fear and gloom*
> *To me it is a pleasant spot—it*
> *is my husband's tomb.*

In 1880 a stonecutter took enough pride in his work to advertise it on his spouse's gravestone:

> Here lies Jane Smith, wife of
> Thomas Smith, marble cutter.
> This monument was erected by
> her husband as a tribute to
> her memory
> and a specimen of his work.
> Monuments of the same style
> 350 dollars.

But an enterprising young widow had already gone him one better on a stone reported from Lincoln, Maine:

> Sacred to the Memory of Mr. Jared
> Bates who Died Aug. the 6th 1800.
> His widow aged 24 who mourns as
> one who can be comforted lives at
> 7 Elm street this village and pos-
> sesses every qualification for a
> good Wife.

Over the years when it was fashionable to relate the manner in which a person left this world, some strange and ironic accounts were chiselled onto stone. There is a strong colonial imprint on epitaphs that tell of men killed by Indian arrows or whales; or "instantly killed by a stagecoach passing over him"; or "by the accidental discharge of a cannon"; or "Casually Drowned in the Proud Waters of the Scungamug River." As remote in thought as in time is the ghastly story engraved on a a stone in Montague, Massachusetts:

> In Memory of Mr. Elijah Bardwell
> who died Janry 26th 1786 in ye 27th
> Year of his Age having but a few days
> surviv'd ye fatal Night when he was
> flung from his Horse & drawn by ye Stirrup
> 26 rods along ye path as appear'd by ye place
> where his hat was found & where he had
> Spent ye whole following severe cold night
> treading ye Snow in a small circle

Common ailments were everywhere, enough of them fatal to keep the stonecutters busy. Fevers carried off young and old alike. Men died gloriously as soldiers fighting Indian battles and in the War for Independence. But they also died of occupational hazards.

One man was "exploded in a powder mill," and another was "Casually Killed by his Wagon"; sailors were "Lost at Sea"; men tumbled from heights; and one "at a barn raising fell down from the roof." Still another dared temptation: "that Cherry Tree of luscious fruit beguiled him too high. A branch did break and down he fell and broke his neck."

With the coming of industrialism the mills provided a catchall of unusual accidents:

> Solomon Towslee Jr
> Who was kill'd in Pownal
> Vt. July 15, 1846, while
> repairing to Grind a sithe
> on a stone atach'd to the
> Gearing in the Woollen
> Factory. he was entangled.
> his death was sudden & awful.

A philosophical stone in Harvard, Massachusetts, cites the mysterious machinations of fate:

> In memory of
> Capt. Thomas Stetson
> Who was killed by the fall of
> a tree Nov. 28 1820 AE. 68
>
> Nearly 30 years he was master
> of a vessel and left that
> employment at the age of
> 48 for the less hazardous
> one of cultivating his farm.
> Man is never secure from
> the arrest of death.

The accusing finger stabbed at some ad man after a young lady "was fatally Burned. . . . by the explosion of a lamp Filled with R. F. Danforth's Non-Explosive Burning Fluid."

Women gentled America's rugged frontiers, and when a man's beloved helpmate "exchanged worlds," only the purest and most heartfelt sentiments were directed to her gravestone. A widower's honest tribute stated simply: "She was more than I expected." But there were exceptions, of course, and if the oft-quoted stone actually exists, a truly vindictive husband finally got his revenge:

> *Here lies my wife*
> *A Slattern and Shrew*
> *If I said I missed her*
> *I should lie here, too!*

Another's intention may have been nobler, but the words on a Keene, New Hampshire, monument arouse doubts:

> *Tears cannot restore her*
> *Therefore I weep.*

Many women died in childbirth; stones for mother and babe are found throughout New England, dating from the earliest times to the turn of the twentieth century. Childbed fever took a dreadful toll. Death approached in many disguises; one young lady "fell from a chaise," and another, while "on a journey in pursuit of health, died suddenly of a Violent Hectick complaint." Besides being exposed to the dangers of frontier life, women suffered more than their share of debilitating diseases, "consumption" prominent among them. A woman in Groton, Massachusetts, was "removed by a dysentery"; not far away a man "died of a bellyache." A memorial slab on Plymouth's Burial Hill tells how Bathsheba James was "Kill'd instantaneously in a Thunder storm by the Electrich fluid of Lightning."

Children fared no better than their elders. From the numerous headstones marking the graves of infants one would assume that it was the fortunate child indeed who persisted to his majority. A typical sentiment states ruefully:

> *From Death's arrest no*
> *age is free*
> *Young children too may die.*

There was little protection against the communicative diseases of childhood, and often an epidemic wiped out an entire family overnight. How discouraging for William and Sarah Langley of Newport, Rhode Island, whose six children, three of them their mother's namesakes, lost their tenuous holds on life, each before the grief for the last had been dispelled! They are commemorated on a multiple stone — six cherubs' heads joined in a row, crowning their respective epitaphs and chiselled from a single slab of slate.

Untimely ends—the most ordinary seems to have been by drowning—were often symbolized by fallen blossoms and described in painful detail: for a young girl "By boiling cyder she was slain"; a boy "kicked in the head by a mule"; another "killed by a cart wheel pass-ing over his head." A most untoward fate was reserved for Jonathan Tute, aged fourteen, of Vernon, Vermont, who left this earthly sphere in 1763:

> *Behold the amazing alteration*
> *Effected by Inoculation*
> *The means Employed his Life to save*
> *Hurried Him Headlong to the Grave.*

Stonecutters sometimes depicted the instruments of death in their carvings. Arrows, upturned boats, wagon wheels, axes, and fallen trees need no words to tell their stories. In Pepperell Center, Massachusetts, the startled figure of little Aaron Bowers, "Instantly killed by a Stock of boards," remains forever transfixed with arms upraised as the timbers bear him down.

Yankees were of necessity jacks-of-all-trades, so that tombstone carving was not necessarily a full-time occupation. Many of these often anonymous artists were farmers, blacksmiths, cobblers, quarry owners, or even sailors, who picked up chisel and mallet as the occasion demanded. The few available records show that certain of them worked for very long periods—more than half a century in a few cases—and achieved a tremendous output. As untrained artists these men were seldom influenced by what the stonecutter in the next village was carving. It is interesting to note that the nature of the stone largely determined the style in which the image was carved. While the coarser marble and sandstones were ideal for the somewhat heavier designs, the smooth, close-grained slate permitted finer lines and more delicate carving. The cutters clung stubbornly to their individualism, each man employing his own motif in one form or another throughout his career.

So little significance was accorded gravestone carving during colonial times that it is exceptional even to find it mentioned among contemporary writers. Yet it recorded history in a very permanent way for a God-fearing, tough-minded people who shrank neither from duty nor death. These old New Englanders cultivated the simple virtues and pleasures and lived out their lives according to stern, unyielding principles. They believed in honesty and hard work, and they held steadfastly to the strength of their convictions. They endured and died secure in faith; that is the sermon in these stones.

Avon Neal and his wife, Ann Parker, tend fruitful vineyards of Americana at their home in North Brookfield, Massachusetts. Their article on ephemeral folk figures appeared in our April, 1970, number, and their gravestone rubbings have been widely hailed and exhibited. A limited edition of one of their original rubbings (not shown here) is available, framed and shipped, to our readers at $55. Orders or requests for more information should be addressed to The Publisher, AMERICAN HERITAGE, 551 Fifth Avenue, New York, N.Y. 10017.

HOW TO SCORE FROM FIRST ON A SACRIFICE

By JAMES "COOL PAPA" BELL
with JOHN HOLWAY

Editor's note: For many years professional baseball contained a shadowland in which some of the finest players in the game spent their athletic careers earning hardly any money and precious little fame. These players, of course, were black men, barred from organized baseball by an unwritten but seemingly unbreakable agreement that the big leagues were for white men only. In 1947 the late Branch Rickey smashed that barrier, once and for all, by bringing in Jackie Robinson to play for the Brooklyn Dodgers. Since the color line was erased, the talented Negro ballplayer has been able to gain the headlines and the high salary brackets; the years in which organized baseball pretended that he did not exist are over.

The big-league players themselves had known all along that he existed. Over and over, after the regular season ended, white all-star teams entered the shadowland to play one or another of the Negro professional teams, often enough getting roundly whipped for their pains; and the big-leaguers readily confessed that among the underpaid black professionals they saw some players who were good enough to be stars on any team, white or black. For years the fabulous pitcher Satchel Paige was legendary. He was in his forties when the color line was erased—an old man, as ballplayers go—but he was still good enough to win a place on the Cleveland Indians and to stay in the majors for a number of years.

One of the black stars who was a little too old to follow in Paige's footsteps was James "Cool Papa" Bell, whom some observers consider the fastest man ever to play baseball—Paige once remarked that Bell was so fast "he could turn out the light and jump in bed before it got dark." Bell played baseball for twenty-nine years, and the most money he ever got was $220 a month. Today he is a night watchman in the St. Louis city hall, and in the following article he tells what it was like in the black leagues of the old days, when teams like the Washington Homestead Grays, the St. Louis Stars, the Chicago American Giants, the Black Yankees, the Lincoln Giants, and the Kansas City Monarchs played in games the ordinary newspaper reader rarely learned about.

What it was like . . . well, you watched all the angles. A few years ago, long after the color barrier had been broken, Cool Papa gave some advice to a rising black star named Maury Wills, who was setting records as a base stealer for the Los Angeles Dodgers. Have the batters who followed him (said Bell) stand far back in the box when Wills got to first and hold their bats back as far as they could. "What does that make the catcher do?" asked Bell. "Move back a step, right? That gives you one more step advantage in beating that ball to second."

Said Wills: "I never thought of that."

Just a bit of lore from the black leagues, where a man had to think of everything.

I was born in 1903 in Starkville, Mississippi, so I was sixty-six last May [1969], and in all I played twenty-nine years summer ball and twenty-one years winter ball. I started playing at sixteen, when I came to St. Louis in 1919 with my four brothers who were playing for the Compton Hills Cubs in the old City League. I made thirty-five to forty dollars a week at the packing house and twenty dollars on Sunday to play ball. It was more than I could make playing ball full time.

In 1922 I was ready to quit baseball. I figured it was time to get a steady job, but the East St. Louis Cubs needed a pitcher to throw against the old St. Louis Stars of the Negro league and they asked me to come out for just one more game. I beat the Stars, and they made me such a good offer that I decided to stick with baseball. When they saw how I could run and throw, they made me an outfielder. I was a natural right-handed batter, but I was a switch-hitter.

They thought I'd be afraid of the crowds, but I said, "Don't worry about it. I've played before crowds on the sand lots—we used to draw ten to eleven thousand people." And they said, "Oh, that guy, he's taking it cool, isn't he?" So they called me Cool Bell. But my manager said, "We've got to add something to it; we'll call him Cool Papa." That's what everyone called me. Most people don't know my real name's Jim.

What a team we had: Quincy Troupe, High-pockets Trent, Mule Suttles, George Giles, Leroy Matlock, Newt Allen, Willie "Devil" Wells, Frog Reddus, Dewey Creacy . . . We played at the park at Compton Avenue and Market Street by the old car barns. We had a lot of fun. And we had a lot of ballplayers better than some of those in the majors today. But some of our owners didn't think we were good enough to play in the majors. They said, "You'd have to learn a whole new system in the majors." That shows how much *they* knew about baseball!

The first time I played against the big-leaguers was against the Detroit Tigers in 1922. I was nineteen then. Cobb and Heilmann didn't play. Cobb had played against a Negro team in Cuba in 1910 and got beat and said he'd never play against us again. But Howard Ehmke pitched. We beat them two out of three. After that Judge Landis, the commissioner, wouldn't let them play a Negro team under their real names. They had to call themselves all-stars. Then if they got beat, we couldn't say we beat a big-league team. For five years we played a postseason series against the Cardinals-Browns all-stars, and they didn't win one series.

We didn't play baseball like they play in the major leagues. We played "tricky baseball." When we played

At right: James "Cool Papa" Bell as he looked in 1942 when he was center fielder for the all-black Chicago American Giants.

U.P.I.

the big-leaguers after the regular season, our pitchers would curve the ball on the 3-2. They'd say, "What, are you trying to make us look bad?" We'd bunt and run and they'd say, "Why are you trying to do that in the first inning?" When we were supposed to bunt, they'd come in and we'd hit away. Oh, we played tricky baseball.

That's why we beat the major-league teams. It's not that we had the best men, but in a short series we could outguess them. Baseball is a guessing game. The major-leaguers would play for one big inning. They go by "written baseball." But there's so much "unwritten baseball." When you use it, they say it's unorthodox.

In our league if a guy was on first and had a chance to go to third, he'd go just fast enough to make the outfielder throw. That way the batter could take second, you see. We'd go into third standing up so the third baseman couldn't see the throw coming and it might go through him. Jackie Robinson learned that from some old players he saw in the Negro leagues. Sometimes you can teach a guy something and he can do it better than you.

The Chicago American Giants had the smartest players you ever saw. They used to bat in a run on a base on balls. If they had a man on third and the batter walked, he'd just trot easy-like down to first and the man on third would just sort of stand there, looking at the stands. At the last minute the batter would cut out for second as fast as he could go; the coach would yell, "Heh, look at that!" The pitcher would whirl around, the guy on third would light out for home, and like as not they wouldn't get anybody out.

I could score from second on a long fly. I've even scored from first on a sacrifice. And I scored from first base on singles lots of times. If the ball isn't hit straight at the outfielder, I'd score. You have to be heads up and watch those things. Or I'd stand back from the plate and chop down on the ball. That's something I learned from the old players. By the time the ball comes down, they can't throw me out.

Stealing home, now that's a dangerous job. I didn't do that too often. You've got to have a good man at bat. And you have to watch the pitcher. When he's working with a windup, as soon as he brings his arm down, that's the time to go. By the time he can bring his arm up again to throw, he can't get you.

You had to know how to steal signs, too. Buck Leonard, our first baseman, was a great hitter, but he didn't hit the curve ball as well as he did the fast ball. I said, "If you knew what was coming, could you hit the ball?" He said, "Yeah." I said, "Well, I bet I can tell you every time a curve's coming. If it's a curve and I'm on first, I'll stand with my hands on my knees. If it's a fast ball, I'll stand straight up. And if I don't know, I'll sort of swing

The fabulous pitcher Satchel Paige was one of those who finally made it to the big leagues—in middle age. He is shown here in 1941, warming up, pregame, for the Kansas City Monarchs.

my arms to say I didn't catch it."

How did I do it? It's easy. Every time a curve is coming, what would the catcher do? He'd move his right foot over a little to be ready to catch it, wouldn't he? I remember the 1964 World Series, the Cardinals and the Yankees, I kept telling the guy next to me, "It's a curve, it's a fast ball." Heck, all I did was watch the catcher.

Earl Whitehill was the toughest big-league pitcher I ever faced. In 1929 we beat the major-league all-stars six out of eight games, and Whitehill beat us both times. The other pitchers were George Uhle and Willis Hudlin. I ran the bases against them the same as I did any other time. If it was time to steal, I'd steal.

Now Pepper Martin of the Cardinals was a pretty good base runner. He ran kind of wild in the World Series in 1931, when he stole five bases. I played against him in 1930 on the Pacific coast. When we played those fellows, they'd come and ask us how we did this or that, and I told Pepper how to get a lead off the pitcher. If you have a catcher with a great arm, you have to get a bigger lead. You can't steal on the catcher much, it's with the pitcher you've got to get the jump. A lot of people don't know this—you can't outrun that ball.

When you get a hit, some people are satisfied if they get a single. But if you run hard, just like you're trying to beat out a bunt, and make your turn at first, if the outfielder has to go over to get the ball, you can go to second. That's how you take your extra base, by hustling all the time. And if you're stealing second, don't be satisfied. Look up, the infielder might miss the ball and you can get up and go to third. A lot of players expect the coaches to tell them, but the coach can't think as fast as the player can.

Well, after Martin had that good year in the Series the next year, he gave all the credit to me for stealing all those bases. They asked him if colored players could play in the majors, and he told them about playing against me and how I had helped him.

The best year I ever had on the bases was 1933. I stole one hundred and seventy-five in about one hundred and eighty to two hundred ball games, all of them against other Negro league teams.

In 1935 I played against Rogers Hornsby's all-stars in Mexico. They had Jimmy Foxx, Rogers Hornsby, Boob McNair, and Max Bishop in the infield, Heinie Manush and Doc Cramer in the outfield, Steve O'Neill catching, and Whitehill pitching. It takes about a week to acclimate to the altitude and they'd been down there about two weeks while we'd just arrived, but we had them beat, 6-4, with two out in the ninth, when Manush was safe on first. Foxx took a 3-2 count and then he got a ball up around his letters and hit it into the bleachers for a home run. The umpire called the game. The sun was up in the sky, but they called the game. That night we all had dinner at an American restaurant, and Foxx told us that the third ball the umpire called was a strike, but he said he wasn't going to argue.

Next day Hornsby hit a ball way over my head. I ran back and caught it over my head. He said, "Come here, Lefty. That was the hardest ball I ever hit. How come you caught it?" Earle Mack, Connie Mack's son, said, "If the door was open, you'd be the first guy I'd hire. I'd pay you seventy-five thousand dollars a year to play ball."

They beat us the last two games, so the next year we said we're going to get a good team and beat Hornsby.

In 1936 we had ten games scheduled against Hornsby in the states. He was slowing up then, but they had him advertised. Satchel Paige never could remember names. In the first game, in Davenport, Iowa, he said, "I want you to tell me when Hornsby comes to bat," so I yelled, "Here's Hornsby." Well, there was a lot of applause, but when the ball hit the catcher's glove, Hornsby would

swing. Satch struck him out two times. Andrew Porter— we used to call him "Pullman Porter"—struck Hornsby out twice, but it was a night game, dark, rainy, and foggy. We got five hits and they got two, but they beat us, 2-1. Johnny Mize got both hits. It was tied, 1-1, and Mize hit a little pop fly behind second. The outfielder ran in to get it and kind of lost the ball in the fog. It was wet and he threw it into left field and Mize went home.

Bobby Feller was just coming up then, and he pitched three innings against us in Des Moines. We got only one hit off him and no runs, but we beat them after he left, 5-2 or 5-3. We beat them a double-header in Denver, came back to Des Moines and beat them again, and they just cancelled the last five games.

I remember one series against Dizzy Dean's all-stars, about 1937 or '38. We opened in York, Pennsylvania, and in the first inning we got four runs off Diz. I hit, Jerry Benjamin hit, Leonard walked, and Josh Gibson hit the ball over the fence. Next time Gibson hit another four-run homer. The people started booing and Diz went into the outfield for a while. He hated to just take himself out of a game. Satchel Paige was pitching for us, and we beat them 13-0.

In New York I got two doubles off Diz in one game. When Gibson came up with me on second, Diz kept telling the outfield, "Get back, get back." Jimmy Ripple was playing center field. He said, "How far do you want me to get back?" But Diz just said, "Get back, get back." It was a scoreless tie. Gibson hit a fly deep to Ripple. I rounded third and made my turn, and Dick Lundy, who was coaching at third, yelled, "Stop." But the shortstop was just getting the throw from Ripple, so I started for home.

The catcher caught the ball high and I slid in—and the umpire called me out. The umpire said, "Look, you don't do that against a big-league team—score from second on an outfield fly." So he called me out.

That winter this guy Trujillo was running the Dominican Republic, only he was having some troubles. He figured since his people liked baseball so much, if he came up with a top-notch team they wouldn't want to see him lose his job. So he imported a bunch of us from the States. There was Paige and Gibson, George Perkins, Samuel Bankhead, Orlando Cepeda's daddy, and me. We didn't know we were being used for a political reason until we got there. Then Trujillo told us if we didn't win the title we would be executed. Some of our boys got so nervous they couldn't play. But we won. Otherwise I probably wouldn't be here to tell about it.

I led the Washington Homestead Grays in hitting for three years. In 1944 I hit .407. In 1945 I was sick, I had a stiff arm, I couldn't throw, I couldn't run. I hit .308, the lowest I ever hit in my life. In 1946 my arm had loosened up and my legs, and I hit .411.

I gave Monte Irvin my batting title. He was our best young player at the time, and he was trying to get into the National League. He hit .389, but they reversed it to read .398. They gave Irvin the batting championship; they said I hadn't played enough games. The fans were mad, but they didn't know what we were trying to do. We were trying to give Irvin the batting championship so he could get a tryout in the majors. After the season was over they were supposed to give me two hundred dollars for giving Irvin my batting title, but they never did give me the two hundred dollars.

Now Jackie Robinson surprised me. He played better in the majors than I thought he would. In 1945 he was

Faces from the old days—the St. Louis Stars, from a photo made probably in the 1930's. Bell is in the front row, fourth from right.

with the Monarchs and we were playing them in Wilmington. Frank Duncan, our manager, came to me and said, "Robinson wants to play in organized ball. He wants to play shortstop." But he couldn't play shortstop. He would have made it at first base, second base, or third base, but not shortstop.

If he missed his chance, I don't know how long we'd go before we'd get another chance. Because, you know, he'd tried out up there in Boston, and they'd turned him down. That's what had been happening all the time. They'd have a tryout and then say, "We didn't see anybody worthwhile." Well, we wanted to show Jackie that he should try out at another position.

Sam Bankhead, Dan's brother, was with the Grays then. We looked at Robinson, and Sam said, "I want you to hit the ball to his right." I was leadoff, and the first time I did it, Jackie caught the ball all right, but you've got to catch it and throw in one motion. Jackie had to take two extra steps. He couldn't backhand it

and pivot. He couldn't throw me out. The next time up I walked two times and stole off him both times. I'd step right over his hands, or slide past him and reach back and touch the base. Now the umpire would call you out, but in our days we played "tricky baseball." I stole four times that night. But Robinson was fast, too. We just played back on him anyway. We just wanted to see him run. Sam Jethroe could outrace him, but Robinson would steal more bases.

In 1948 Satchel Paige wanted me to manage the Kansas City Monarchs' farm team. He told me, "You never made money in baseball; this may be your chance to make some money." So I said, "Here's a boy I want, Elston Howard, just out of high school here in St. Louis." I recommended him to Buck O'Neill, the Monarchs' manager. And I said, "I've got another boy I want in school in Dallas, Ernie Banks." O'Neill said he didn't need a shortstop. But I said, "Look at him work out," and that's how they found him. Later I offered Howard and Banks to the Browns, to Mr. Peters, who was director of their minor-league system. But he didn't want them. The Cards also tried out Howard, and they didn't take him, either, and I said, "If they don't want *those* two boys, who *do* they want?"

That year was also the last time I ever scored from first on a sacrifice. I'd done that many times, but this time I was forty-five years old. We were playing the major-league all-stars in California, and I was hitting eighth. I got on base, and Satchel came up and sacrificed me to second. Well, Bob Lemon came off the mound to field it, and I saw that third base was open because the third baseman had also charged in to field it. Roy Partee, the catcher, saw me going to third, so he went down the line to cover third and I just came on home past him. Partee called, "Time, time!" but the umpire said, "I can't call time, the ball's still in play," so I scored.

I retired after that. I figured it was time to find a steady job before I was too old. I went to work for the city, first as a custodian and then as a night watchman. Even after I quit, people still were after me to play. But my legs were bad, I had varicose veins, I couldn't run. I got tired, you know. That was in 1951. Heck, I was forty-eight years old at the time!

People told me I should have tried for a big-league job just for the money, but I couldn't do it just for a paycheck. I never had any money, so I never worried about it. I just didn't want the fans to boo me, and if I had played at that age they sure would have. Sometimes pride is more important than money.

Now they've got Roy Campanella heading a committee to name Negro players to the Hall of Fame. But he only knows those he played against. He never saw some of the older ones. If some of these fellows don't get into the Hall of Fame, it's no use putting anyone in there. There were two or three hundred of those fellows to put in there. I'd put in four, five, six at one time.

Now they're trying to set it up so Paige and Josh Gibson get in. In pitching, I'd put Paige in with Smokey Joe Williams, Bullet Joe Rogan, and Stringbean Williams. Those guys were fast, they were smart, and they knew how to pitch. In our league they threw the spitter, the screwball, emery ball, shine ball—that means vaseline ball; there was so much vaseline on it, it made you blink your eyes on a sunny day. Then they threw the mud ball —the mud on its seams made it sink. The emery ball would break either up or down, but if a sidearmer threw it and didn't know what he was doing, it could sail right into the hitter. It was a dangerous pitch.

Well, Satch could pitch right in there with those boys, and they weren't any faster than he was, but Satch made the majors, so now they're going to pick him over everybody. Satchel was the fastest pitcher I ever saw. He was so fast you couldn't time him. He had this hesitation

Bell, at right, chats with the great Josh Gibson before a game played for Dictator Rafael Trujillo in the Dominican Republic. The team was told it would be shot if it lost. It did not lose.

pitch. When he was a kid, he'd fight with a gang, and a little guy would get behind a tree and stick his head out and duck when Satchel threw at him. So Satchel developed this hesitation pitch. He'd make a move to throw, the kid would duck, then Satchel would really pitch and hit the kid when he peeked out again. There's nothing in the world against that in the rule books, but after he went to Cleveland he was fooling those big-league batters. They didn't want that, so they outlawed it.

Josh Gibson I'd put in with a group of four or five catchers. Some of those catchers might do more than he could. The long ball was the only thing he could do better. Gibson wasn't the best defensive catcher. There were two things Campanella could do better than him: catch pop flies and receive the ball. But Gibson was a smart catcher. He was smart and he was fast. Sometimes he just dropped the ball on purpose to get some guy to run. And he threw a light ball. You could catch it without a glove. Campanella threw it like a brick.

I was the man who kept records on Gibson—sometimes they didn't even keep a box score. But when I got with the Pittsburgh Crawfords, I started to count Gibson's homers—seventy-two in one year, 1933. Josh hit one over the center-field fence in Griffith Stadium. The longest ball ever hit in Yankee Stadium, Josh hit it. He hit it against the back of the left-field bullpen—almost out of the park.

Take Larry Brown, who used to play for Nashville, Memphis, and Philadelphia. He was a great little catcher. Cobb happened to see him play, and they were talking about getting the colored into baseball. Brown was a very light fellow, and Cobb told them to send him to Cuba and teach him to speak Spanish so they could recruit him. It came out after Cobb died that he said if Brown ever got to the majors, he wanted him on his side, he didn't want to have to run against him.

Did you ever hear of Oscar Charleston? Some people said he was the greatest Negro ballplayer, but John McGraw said he was the greatest *ball*player he'd ever seen. He was a left-handed hitter, but it didn't make any difference—left-handed or right-handed pitchers, he hit them all. Against the major-league all-stars in Mexico in 1935, every time he'd come up with men on base they'd walk him, because they'd heard so much about him.

He was a center fielder like Willie Mays, and I'd have to pick him over Mays. He was a sensational ballplayer like Mays. If they hit the ball high, he'd walk just fast enough to catch it, or he'd turn a flip and then catch it. And he played right behind second base, closer than Mays. But Charleston could go back and get the long balls.

Charleston was one of those rough boys. He had nerve, he'd fight, do anything. Like Ty Cobb. He'd run over you, spike you, tell the pitcher, "Throw it at me, I'll hit it down your throat." I heard that he pulled the hood off a Ku Klux Klansman in Indiana once. I didn't see that myself, but it sounded like him. He wasn't afraid of anything.

Now I couldn't pick an all-time all-star team. It wouldn't be fair. Who would you leave off? Who would I put at third base? Oliver Marcelle was supposed to be the greatest third baseman of all time, but all around, Judy Johnson was better than Marcelle was. Judy was a little fellow, but he could hit, he could throw, and he was smart. He's a scout for the Phillies now. A little later there was Ray Dandridge. They thought he was a Mexican—he was very light—and they went down to

It was Jackie Robinson who broke the big-league color barrier permanently. He wanted to be a shortstop, but it was hard for him to go to his right. As a second baseman he could go left expertly.

scout him, but they found out he was a Negro and they wiped him out.

Now Willie Wells was the greatest shortstop in the world. They were scouting him in Chicago at the Negro East-West game, which is what we used to call our all-star game. But the older fellows would say Pop Lloyd was the greatest. He played against Cobb in Cuba in 1910. Cobb used to spike guys, but our guys were used to that because we did the same thing, so it didn't bother Lloyd. He beat Cobb hitting in one series, and after that Cobb said he never would play against a Negro team anymore. I didn't see Lloyd in his best days, but if any-

one was better than Wells, he had to be perfect.

At second base, who would you pick, Sammy T. Hughes or Bingo Demoss? Demoss played for the Chicago American Giants, smart, a great bunter, and a great runner. He died about a year ago.

In the outfield there was Martin Dihigo, the Cuban—they say he's one of Castro's boys now. Doby Moore of Kansas City, who was shot and killed in 1932, didn't play very long, but he was a long-ball hitter. And Chino Smith, who also died young, could hit that ball hard. Then there was Sam Bennett, who died last year. He gave Tris Speaker pointers on how to play center field.

Those were great times. We used to play a night game Saturday, get in the bus, and play a double-header Sunday and then play another night game Sunday night. You show me a ballplayer in our old league and I'll show you a guy that can sleep standing, sitting, or walking. When I went out East baseball was easier to play than in the West. They'd play only five days a week, so we had time to sit around the lobbies and talk baseball. The rest of the time we'd be cramped up, riding the bus.

The worst was the pay, and it didn't matter who you were playing for. The most I ever made was two hundred and twenty dollars a month. Most of the others were getting ninety to one hundred and twenty-five dollars a month.

During the Depression some of the teams just stopped paying salaries. But the players didn't have anywhere else to work so they stayed. They got expense money, but a lot of times it was so little you didn't have enough money to eat on. And some of the owners were pretty tricky. I remember one team hired me and told me to pay my transportation from St. Louis to Memphis and they'd pay me back. But when I got there they said, "Our players pay their own expenses." And then this guy told me, "And the owner of the club is a dentist and all our players have their teeth fixed here." I didn't have a toothache and I wasn't about to pay a man to fix what didn't need fixing, so I just turned around and went home.

We had some players in our league better than those in the major leagues now, but when the doors were finally open, they were too old. Look at Luke Easter and Sam Jethroe: they were thirty-five.

But I've got no kicks, no regrets. I made my share of money. Of course it would have been nice to play in the majors, but I have my memories.

My greatest thrill? Well, everyone has his own favorite day. But I've got to say my biggest thrill was when they opened the door to the Negro. When they said we couldn't play and we proved that we could, that was the biggest thrill to me. There were more guys before me who didn't have a chance, and I wanted us to prove it to 'em all, black and white alike.

THE CASE
of the
DISAPPEARING
COOK

By MARK SUFRIN

On August 27, 1906, the daughter of Charles Henry Warren, a New York banker, fell sick at the family's rented summer house in Oyster Bay, Long Island. For the first few days the illness was deceptively mild; then the doctor began to note alarming symptoms—a high fever and low pulse rate, nosebleeds, nausea, and diarrhea. A rose-colored rash appeared on the girl's stomach, which was slightly distended and sensitive to any pressure.

The syndrome was classic: the girl had typhoid fever, one of the most contagious of communicable diseases. At the turn of the century thousands of people were stricken in typhoid epidemics, and nearly twenty-three thousand died in the United States in the year 1906 alone.

Within the same week that the girl became ill, five more persons in the household, including Warren's wife, were stricken with typhoid. Experts were brought in to investigate the outbreak and concluded it was due to contagion from the daughter. They could not pinpoint the source of the original infection but said that she had probably contracted the disease from contaminated water or milk, or perhaps spoiled food. There had been no other instance of typhoid in Oyster Bay either before or after the outbreak.

The outbreak might have been forgotten had not George Thompson, the owner of the house, been afraid that it would be impossible to rent it the following sum-

37

DRAWN FOR AMERICAN HERITAGE BY LAWRENCE DI FIORI

mer unless the cause was definitely established. He asked George A. Soper, a sanitary engineer in the New York City Department of Health, to investigate the matter. A well-known epidemic fighter, Soper had been instrumental in setting up emergency health procedures when typhoid epidemics struck Watertown and Ithaca, New York, a few years before.

Retracing the initial investigation, Soper quickly eliminated the usual sources of contamination: the water supply and drainage, the single inside toilet, the cesspools, manure pit, and outside privy. No detail had been overlooked. Frustrated, Soper suddenly sensed that some extraordinary factor had shattered the placid household shortly before the outbreak. He began to concentrate on the possibility of a human carrier, a new theory developed by the noted German bacteriologist Robert Koch. Humans, it was already known, were carriers as long as they were ill themselves and sometimes for several weeks after recovery, when their urine was still highly infectious. Koch, however, believed that outwardly healthy persons also spread the disease, continually breeding the typhoid bacilli within their bodies and discharging the germs in their feces, although they may never have suffered even a high fever. Soper was the first man in America to put the theory to a test.

Because the normal period of typhoid incubation is ten to fourteen days, Soper figured that all the victims in the Warren household were stricken by food or drink taken on or shortly before August 20. He studied the movements of each person without success; no one had left Oyster Bay during the crucial period. However, the Warrens had changed cooks on August 4. The new one, a woman named Mary Mallon, was missing. Mrs. Warren told Soper that she had hired Mary through a New York employment agency that catered to the domestic needs of the well-to-do. Mary was a "pretty good" cook, though not particularly clean and somewhat difficult to talk to. ("Few housekeepers seem to know anything about their cooks," complained Soper.) Mary left without a word about three weeks after the sickness began.

It was little more than a hunch, but from that time Mary Mallon became Soper's prime target. With the determination of a detective, he began to track her down. He already had a good description of her: Mary was about forty years old, tall, with a buxom figure, blond hair, clear blue eyes, and a firm mouth and jaw. But there was little else to go on. Nothing at all was known about her personal life.

Soper started with the employment agency that had referred Mary to the Warrens. He interviewed dozens of people, collected every scrap of information about her, however innocuous, and with painstaking care, reconstructed a patchy mosaic of her working record for the

ten years before she became the Warrens' cook.

In 1897 Mary began working for a family in Mamaroneck, New York. Early in September of 1900 a young houseguest was stricken with typhoid ten days after his arrival. It was thought at first he had contracted the fever during a visit with friends on Long Island, near an army camp where typhoid was prevalent. Mary left Mamaroneck suddenly a few days after the young man became ill.

During the winter of 1901–2 she cooked for a family in Manhattan. On December 9, one month after Mary arrived, a laundress was taken sick with typhoid and removed to a hospital. There was no investigation, and Mary stayed on for a time.

She next turned up in the summer home of J. Coleman Drayton, a New York lawyer, at Dark Harbor, Maine. The first case of typhoid broke out on June 17, 1902, a few weeks after her arrival. Within the next two weeks six more persons in the household fell sick. Only Mary and Drayton, apparently immune because he had once had typhoid, escaped being stricken. Together they nursed the others. Mary remained until the fever was blunted, and the grateful lawyer gave her a fifty-dollar bonus. The investigators' report stated that a maid, the first afflicted, had contaminated a water tank that infected the others. However, there was no explanation of how the maid had caught the disease.

Soper then tracked Mary to the summer estate of Henry Gilsey in Sands Point, Long Island. On June 8, 1904, shortly after her arrival, typhoid felled a laundress who had been on the grounds only ten days. Then three more servants fell ill. Because no one in the Gilsey family was affected, the fever was believed to be rooted in the servants' quarters, which were separated from the main house. One expert, Dr. Robert L. Wilson, the superintendent of hospitals for communicable diseases in the New York City Health Department, was convinced that the laundress had been infected before coming to Sands Point, but he could not determine how she had contracted the disease.

The next two years in Mary's past, until she went to work for the Warrens, were a blank, but in December, 1906, Soper broke a fresh trail. Mary had taken a job in Tuxedo, New York, on September 21, only a few days after vanishing from Oyster Bay. Two weeks after her arrival a laundress collapsed with typhoid. Mary left abruptly on October 27.

The evidence of Mary's implication was now overwhelming: typhoid broke out wherever she worked, and she escaped illness each time and, invariably, ran away when the sickness appeared. Soper was certain that Mary was the innocent victim of her body chemistry—a living culture tube in which the deadly bacilli found a congenial environment, breeding and multiplying. If fore-

Easily enraged, Mary seized a carving fork and frightened off Soper when he first told her that she was probably a typhoid carrier.

warned, she could lead a normal life, with only a few restrictions. More important, Mary had to be found before any further outbreaks occurred, and tests had to be taken to prove that she was a chronic carrier—for if she was, then innumerable others might also unwittingly be carriers. Soper needed specimens of her body waste to confirm his theory.

Mary, however, proved an elusive creature, and the search seemed to be at a dead end. Soper, familiar now with her pattern, believed she was probably somewhere in New York City, still working as a cook for some wealthy family. Then one day in March, 1907, he came face to face with her in a private brownstone on Park Avenue in the Sixties. The owner's daughter was dying of typhoid and a maid was ill with the fever when Soper went by to investigate. He was taken to the kitchen and introduced to Mary.

As she wiped her hands slowly and leaned against the cupboard, Soper calmly began to explain that he suspected her of being a typhoid carrier. It was necessary, he said, to obtain specimens of her blood, urine, and feces. Without warning, Mary grabbed a large carving fork and advanced toward Soper. He fled the house, feeling helpless.

Learning that Mary often spent her nights with a man who lived in a run-down Third Avenue rooming house, Soper decided to confront her again. Accompanied by Dr. Raymond Hoobler, he waited for her at the top of the stairs one evening. Mary got angry the moment she saw him. No sooner had Soper begun telling her that he meant no harm than Mary started shouting that she had never had typhoid nor carried it. She was clean, in perfect health, she insisted, and had no sign or symptom of any disease. There had been no more typhoid where she worked than anywhere else—typhoid was everywhere—Soper was persecuting her. If he knew about Dark Harbor, then he knew she didn't harm the family but had helped them. Didn't Mr. Drayton reward her? Nothing Soper said would swerve her. The two men left as Mary stood at the head of the stairs, cursing after them.

Realizing that it was hopeless to reason with her any longer, Soper appealed to Health Commissioner Thomas Darlington and Dr. Hermann M. Briggs, the department's medical officer. Mary, he said, was "a living culture . . . a proved menace to the community." Under suitable conditions, he declared, "Mary might precipitate a great epidemic." Darlington and Briggs thought that one more attempt should be made to get the specimens peacefully—by someone other than Soper.

On March 18, 1907, Dr. S. Josephine Baker, a Health Department inspector, went to see Mary but had no more success with the unyielding woman than Soper. Mary, her eyes glinting and her jaw set, refused to submit the specimens in a way "that left little room for persuasion or argument."

It took five policemen to subdue Mary when she was arrested. Kicking and screaming, she was rushed off to a hospital, where tests proved that she was "a living culture" of typhoid bacilli.

The following morning, Dr. Baker returned with an ambulance and three policemen. Her superior, Dr. Walter Bensel, assistant sanitary superintendent for Manhattan, had issued a firm order: get the specimens. If Mary resisted, she was to be overpowered and taken to the Willard Parker Hospital for Contagious Diseases, at the foot of East Sixteenth Street.

Leaving the ambulance at the corner, Dr. Baker stationed one officer in front of the house, a second at the back, and, accompanied by the third policeman, approached the basement entrance under the front steps. Mary, on her guard now, opened the door just wide enough to lunge viciously at Dr. Baker with a kitchen fork "like a rapier." The doctor fell back into the officer, who then managed to jam his foot in the doorway as the cook fled toward the rear of the house. When they recovered and reached the kitchen, Mary had vanished. The other servants, out of loyalty, denied seeing her.

Dr. Baker and the officers searched the house for three hours and turned up only a single clue: footprints in the snow outside leading to a chair set by the high fence between the brownstone and the one adjoining it. A search of that building proved fruitless, and Dr. Baker called her superior to report that Mary was gone. Dr. Bensel merely replied, "I expect you to get the specimens or to take Mary to the hospital," and hung up.

Commandeering two more policemen in the street, Dr. Baker resumed the search. After two hours of scouring every possible hiding place, she was ready to give up, wondering how she could face Dr. Bensel, when one of the policemen spotted a piece of blue calico caught in the closet door in the areaway under the high outside front stairway of the second house. A dozen ash cans were stacked in front of the door, evidently put there by the cook's servant friends.

The cans were removed and the door pulled open. Mary sprang from a crouch and came out fighting and cursing ("both of which she could do with appalling efficiency and vigor," the doctor recalled). A big, strong woman, Mary put up a bitter struggle for her freedom. It took all five policemen to finally subdue her and lift her, kicking and screaming, into the ambulance.

"I made another effort to talk to her sensibly," said Dr. Baker, "and asked her again to let me have the specimens, but it was no use. By that time she was convinced that the law was wantonly persecuting her, when she had done nothing wrong. She knew she had never had typhoid fever; she was maniacal in her integrity. There was nothing I could do but take her with us. . . . I literally sat on her all the way to the hospital; it was like being in a cage with an angry lion."

Mary Mallon was locked away in a bare, stark-white isolation ward, classified as a dangerous patient who might attempt escape. She was the charge of Dr. Robert L. Wilson, who had investigated the Sands Point outbreak in 1904, and Dr. William H. Park, chief of the Health Department's bacteriological laboratories.

The first analysis of Mary's feces showed a pure culture of the deadly bacteria. Subsequent examinations for the next eight months disclosed that except for intervals of a few weeks, her body was continually discharging the deadly germs. The tests established, without doubt, that an outwardly healthy person could breed and spread typhoid fever.

Shortly after her arrest, Soper, in a sense her nemesis but with compassion for Mary, visited her at the hospital. She was "fearfully angry-looking" as he spoke:

"Mary, I've come to talk . . . [to] see if between us we cannot get you out of here. . . . You would not be where you are now if you had not been so obstinate. . . . Nobody wants to harm you. You say you have never caused a case of typhoid, but I know you have done so. Nobody thinks you have done it purposely. . . . Many people have been made sick and have suffered a great deal; some have died. . . . You were arrested and brought here and the specimens taken. . . . They proved what I charged. Now you must surely see how mistaken you were. Don't you acknowledge it?"

Mary only glared at Soper as he continued, "Well, I will tell you how you do it. When you go to the toilet, the germs which grow within your body get upon your fingers, and when you handle food in cooking they get on the food. People who eat this food swallow the germs and get sick. If you would wash your hands after leaving the toilet and before cooking, there might be no trouble."

Soper tried to glean some sign in her face that he was breaking through, but Mary remained silent and grim, staring at him with angry eyes. He persisted, saying that the bacteria were probably hatched in her gall bladder and that it should be removed. The operation was difficult and not always successful, but her case called for the most drastic preventive measures.

"You don't need a gall bladder any more than you need an appendix," Soper concluded. "There are many people living without them. . . . I don't know how long the Department of Health intends to keep you here. . . . I can help you. If you will answer my questions. . . . Above all, I want to know if and when you have had typhoid fever, and how many outbreaks and cases you have seen."

Her eyes digging into Soper's, Mary rose from the bed, drew her robe about her, walked into the bathroom, and slammed the door. Refusing to co-operate, she thereafter maintained that the operation was only "a pretext for killing her."

After several weeks at the Willard Parker Hospital,

Mary was transferred to Riverside Hospital on North Brother Island, a bleak, thirteen-acre patch of ground in the East River between Long Island Sound and the roiling waters of Hell Gate. She was eventually allowed to work as a laundress, but otherwise she was cut off from contact with others. Mary Mallon, however, was no spirit to languish without a fight.

Two legal actions to free her were brought against the city. On June 9, 1909, Mary and a lawyer who specialized in medical cases, George Francis O'Neill, appeared before a state supreme court judge. She testified that she had been kept "like a leper," with only a dog for company. Three times a day, she said, a nurse shoved food through her door, then ran away in fright.

O'Neill argued that Mary was being deprived of her freedom without having committed a crime or knowingly having done injury to any person or property. She had been held without a hearing, he pointed out, and was

Five years after her disappearance, Mary—although heavily veiled —was spotted by New York detectives as she entered a friend's home.

apparently under a life sentence, contrary to the United States Constitution. Such action was without precedent in law, he declared.

The judge, however, ruled against Mary's petition. He expressed sympathy but said he was unwilling to take the responsibility for freeing her.

Nearly a month later, on July 22, 1909, another judge denied a writ of habeas corpus, stating that the Health Department had acted within its rights in holding Mary Mallon in custody. As authority he cited sections of the city charter dealing with "imminent peril," as well as the state's health law.

The legal battles attracted much attention. Newspapers dubbed the cook Typhoid Mary, and cartoons depicted her frying typhoid bacilli the size of sausages, or dropping human skulls into a skillet. Some were kinder, viewing Mary as the lonely victim of bad luck, sitting out her life with only a faithful mongrel at her side. *Punch*, the British humor weekly, devoted a column of poetry to her. The notoriety also brought her a suitor, a twenty-eight-year-old Michigan farmer who wrote the Health Department for permission to marry her, confiding that he had once been in an insane asylum but had since been declared mentally sound. The Health Department, meanwhile, had rounded up hundreds of suspected typhoid breeders, concentrating on cooks and dairymen who had come in contact with typhoid victims. Many proved to be chronic carriers but were allowed to return to their homes after pledging not to take any job that entailed contact with food or its preparation. In February, 1910, Mary convinced hospital officials that she, too, was prepared to take special precautions to avoid contaminating others. She promised to give up making her living as a cook and to report to the Health Department every three months.

Almost as soon as she was released, Mary vanished. For five years she drifted from job to job, avoiding work in private homes. She tried running a cheap rooming house but lost money at it. She took in ironing but found that cooking paid better. Carefully staying clear of employment agencies, she found jobs in a Broadway restaurant, several hotels on Long Island, and at a fashionable resort and a sanitarium in New Jersey. In each there were cases of typhoid, but the record was incomplete, and Mary, who sometimes called herself Marie Breshof or Mary Brown, was not identified at the time.

Then, in February, 1915, Soper was called to the Sloane Hospital for Women by Dr. Edwin B. Cragin, head obstetrician and gynecologist. Twenty-five persons, most of them nurses and attendants, had been suddenly stricken with typhoid, a crippling loss for the institution. Two of the victims were dying.

Sloane was one of the best hospitals in New York, a

model of good sanitation. Soper examined the personnel records. A cook had been hired three months before the outbreak. He was told that when the other employees had teasingly called her "Typhoid Mary," she had left without notice. Shown a sample of her handwriting, Soper quickly identified the cook as Mary Mallon.

For the first time, he wondered if there was something mentally wrong with Mary. She had deliberately taken chances with human life in a hospital—"spreading typhoid germs among mothers and babies and doctors and nurses like a destroying angel"—where the risk of being caught and severely punished was greater than anywhere else.

Mary's trail led to New Jersey, then to Long Island, where city detectives spotted her, heavily veiled, carrying a bowl of gelatin to a friend's house. Police surrounded the house, while others slipped inside. This time Mary had little chance to struggle. On March 27, 1915, Mary was returned to North Brother Island.

The staff at Riverside Hospital tried to rehabilitate and cure her. Dr. Park experimented with a kind of hyperimmunization, feeding and injecting Mary with six billion typhoid bacilli. She was given a billion by hypodermic and supplied with the rest of the dosage in pills that were to be taken at stated intervals. Mary either threw the pills away or hid them; anyway, the immunization failed. Rejecting any attempts of help, she doomed herself to the life of an outcast. Whatever rights she once possessed as an "innocent" carrier were lost now. She was dangerous, an incorrigible—and was to be kept in almost complete isolation for the rest of her life.

At least fifty-three cases of typhoid and three deaths were attributed to Mary Mallon, a small tally compared with that of other carriers who were found. But how many outbreaks or epidemics she actually touched off, or how many sick and dead she accounted for in all, would never be known. Mary herself never disclosed a word about her past, only that she had been born in the United States. She continued to refuse to answer any questions or to have her photograph taken. And she never expressed any remorse for all the suffering she caused.

Almost forty-eight years old, a great deal heavier, and with much of her remarkable energy gone, Mary drew into herself, a lost and sullen woman. For a long time she responded to any gesture of friendship with "almost pathological anger." A less intelligent and dedicated staff might have given up on Mary, but the nurses and doctors at Riverside Hospital slowly drew her from her shell. In her fifties she was given a job in the hospital laboratories and proved herself an intelligent aide. Mary learned the intricate work, read every book available on the island, and sent to the city for textbooks. Paid sixty dollars a month as an inmate staff member, she prepared slides for the pathologists, kept records, and generally helped in the laboratory. Occasionally she was allowed to go into the city for a few hours alone. She found solace in religion and became a devout Roman Catholic.

In 1923 the city gave her a home of her own on North Brother Island, a comfortable, one-room cottage with its own small plot of lawn and two elm trees. From its porch she could look north to the gas tanks on the Bronx shore, south to sleazy apartment houses and factories in Astoria, and east to the city prison on Riker's Island. An occasional ferryboat glided past in the sludgy waters, and at night the river lapped against the rocks in an unnerving beat. In fair weather she often entertained friends from the hospital on the porch. But when mealtime came, the guests departed. There was no talk about it, no jokes; Mary cooked and ate alone. When alone, she sewed, took walks, or read (Dickens was her favorite author). She was examined periodically, but the virulence in her body never lessened.

On Christmas morning, 1932, a deliveryman found Mary on the floor of her cottage, paralyzed by a stroke. She lingered six more years, a helpless invalid, in the hospital ward. On November 11, 1938, after spending nearly half her seventy years in confinement, she died. That night, her coffin was carried from the hospital through a side exit, taken to the small pier, and loaded aboard a launch. The death certificate was handed to the captain, and he signed a receipt for his cargo. Then the craft cut into the dark river, heading toward the Bronx shore.

The next morning a short Requiem Mass was held in St. Luke's Roman Catholic Church. Nine mourners attended, but none would disclose their identity to reporters. No one followed her coffin to St. Raymond's Cemetery in the Bronx.

Always an enigma to others, Mary Mallon remained in memory only the symbol of pestilence called Typhoid Mary. When she died, there were 349 chronic typhoid carriers registered in the city, only one of whom the Health Department felt it necessary to keep isolated. The incidence of typhoid, much to Soper's credit, was down to a few hundred cases a year.

Soper, who later was a pioneer in the campaign for cancer research, wrote what could have served as a fitting epitaph for Mary:

"Surely a mysterious, noncommunicative, self-reliant, abundantly courageous person; a character apart, by nature and circumstance, strangely chosen to bear the burden of a great lesson to the world."

Mark Sufrin is a free-lance writer who has also directed film documentaries and been a motion-picture critic and lecturer.

From John Bull to Uncle Sam:

HOW TO RUN AN EMPIRE

By JONATHAN AITKEN

Before advising Americans on how to manage their empire, it is first necessary to convince them that their empire exists. This is no easy task, for the comment of the nineteenth-century Cambridge historian Sir John Seely, who said of the British Empire that it was acquired "in a fit of absence of mind," could, until very recently, be far more appropriately applied to the present imperial role of the United States. Until the Vietnam conflict blew up into a heated domestic political controversy, most Americans were so absent-minded about their dominion over far-flung palm and pine that the schoolboy's question, "Does the United States have an empire?" could truthfully be answered, "Yes, but they've forgotten about it."

Such forgetfulness, though genuine, cuts little ice among the previous bearers of the White Man's Burden, for we British know an empire when we see one. Although today the globe is not coloured with large splashes of the American equivalent of imperial red, yet by skilfully allowing the local natives to enjoy the forms of power while Washington controls the substance, the twentieth century's most prominent anticolonialists have made it respectable to occupy a chain of world-wide military garrisons and even to possess overseas colonies. Admittedly, Alaska is overland and was bought from Russia, but it is certainly not contiguous to the continental United States. As for Hawaii and Puerto Rico, Okinawa and other former Japanese islands in the Pacific, the war-dependent economies of South Vietnam and Thailand, the myriad trust territories in Micronesia, the puppet state of Panama, and the cunningly manipulated but independent Philippines—here is an empire in all its untarnished trappings. A nostalgic Englishman can only envy this phenomenon and admire the dexterity by which the world is mesmerized into believing it isn't there.

But the American empire was far more invisible than it is today when Englishmen began giving the United States imperial advice. The first and perhaps most distinguished of these mentors was Rudyard Kipling. After the United States took over the administration of the Philippine Islands following the Spanish-American War, Kipling in 1899 published a famous poem, "The White Man's Burden," which was directly aimed at the new American imperialists. It has proved so prophetic that perhaps three stanzas are worth quoting:

> Take up the White Man's burden—
> Send forth the best ye breed—
> Go bind your sons to exile
> To serve your captives' need;
> To wait in heavy harness,
> On fluttered folk and wild—
> Your new-caught, sullen peoples,
> Half-devil and half-child.
>
> Take up the White Man's burden—
> The savage wars of peace—
> Fill full the mouth of Famine
> And bid the sickness cease;
> And when your goal is nearest
> The end for others sought,
> Watch Sloth and heathen Folly
> Bring all your hope to nought.
>
> Take up the White Man's burden—
> And reap his old reward:
> The blame of those ye better,
> The hope of those ye guard . . .
> Comes now, to search your manhood
> Through all the thankless years,
> Cold, edged with dear-bought wisdom
> The judgment of your peers!

Reading those lines seventy-one years ago, many Americans must have pooh-poohed them as hysteria. For Kipling was striking at the great American beliefs that it is possible to be generous and not to be despised, to rule and not to be disliked, to be powerful and not to be hated. Unfortunately time has vindicated Kipling's cynicism more than American idealism. Faced with Return Okinawa riots by Japanese students, protest marches by Guam islanders, and anti-American demonstrations throughout South America, Kipling's phrases have a painful ring of truth.

But having scored the debating point that British advice to the American empire is not to be taken lightly, let us turn away from post-mortems and towards the future. It is a perfect moment to do this, for the end of the Vietnam war will be either the finest or the darkest hour for American imperialism. When the armistice is signed on the 50th parallel, whatever the communiqués may say, America's enemies will assert that the new empire has lost a war, lost face, and lost the confidence and esteem of her allies. Many of those allies will be secretly and spitefully delighted. For America herself it will be the parting of the ways. For nearly thirty years she will have moved away from her homely traditions and down the imperial road. This is the new empire's first reverse. All the old Yankee prejudices, all the latent isolationism of the early years, all the diverse forces which lead the new generation to revolt against society, will be brought into play, and there will be immense pressures to start a return to the cosy assurance of the American womb. Why, it will be asked, was America ever tempted to go back to the bad old struggles from which the early fathers had with such travail escaped? Surely the whole *raison d'être* of the nation was to create a haven away from political entanglements for the "huddled masses yearning to breathe free"? What was the Monroe Doctrine but a barrier against outside interference with the American dream? And where was the American dream to be realised except in America? It will be a testing moment, perhaps the supremely testing moment of the century. The British Empire underwent a similar moment when, in December, 1805, Napoleon overthrew Austria at Austerlitz, and all Europe, until then subsidised and succoured by England, was in French hands. In one agonised outburst, Pitt ordered the map of Europe to be rolled up; but only a few months later, just before he died, he confidently declared in a speech at the Guildhall in 1805, "England has saved herself by her exertions, and will, as I trust, save Europe by her example." It is not too far-fetched to argue, against the background of increasingly militant Communist expansionism in Asia, that the situation of 1806 is about to be with the Western world again.

The time for advice has arrived. If America is not to lose her imperial sway, she must retain her empire. To do so, she will certainly have to reconsider some attitudes. She may even be obliged to reform some institutions. Let us take the empire first, the threefold empire— the territories outside the continental United States, the military bastions around the world, and the great golden calf reflecting the American way of life.

Keep, I would say to Americans, all your overseas territories. If weak nations ask for your protection, give it. Do not surrender Guam. Do not negotiate a transfer of Guantánamo. Keep a firm hold of the Panama Canal. Maintain your bases in Subic Bay and in the Ryukyu

CONTINUED ON PAGE 76

Our illustration, which entirely suits this article, was drawn by Joseph Keppler for Puck *in 1899, when America began to enter the imperialism business overseas following the Spanish-American War.*

The "memory paintings" of a lady now ninety-four celebrate
the life of rural Texas as it was when she grew up there

AUNT CLARA'S LUMINOUS WORLD

Clara McDonald Williamson in 1964

Inevitably, most of the personal records of life on the American frontier that have come down to us are masculine and epic in tone. Guns and battles and duels and expeditions, cattle drives and buffalo hunts and the carving out of empires —men were the ones who forged that drama, and for the most part the ones who had their say about it. So the quiet, hard, meaningful daily life of village and house and field that went on behind it is sometimes hard for us to glimpse.

In my corner of the world, the north-central part of Texas, this gap is filled in part by the paintings of a gifted and perceptive eyewitness, Clara McDonald Williamson, generally known in the art world as Aunt Clara. Mrs. Williamson, now ninety-four and still alertly interested in the world that was and is, did not begin painting until she was nearly seventy. Most of her important paintings—classified as primitive or naïve, like those of Grandma Moses, by people who classify such things—are what she calls "memory pictures." They depict sharp moments and scenes recollected from her early life in the little town of Iredell, Texas, where she was born in the fall of 1875, less than two decades after the community had taken shape.

Astraddle the North Bosque River on the western edge of the Texas Grand Prairie, Iredell is about seven miles from the ninety-eighth meridian, often identified as the division line between East and West, woodland and plains. It has hot summers and cool winters, with good, dependable rain most years. The rolling prairies roundabout and the narrow flat bottomlands along the streams are padded with excellent limestone soil, where man's use of them has not been ruinous. Rising three hundred feet or so above them here and there are steep, flat-topped hills and ridges, most of them dark with cedar and scrub oak and known locally as mountains, which keep the landscape from monotony and preserve, in the exposed strata of their slopes, a record of the ancient processes of inundation, deposition, upheaval, climatic change, and erosion by which the land was made into what it is.

Before white settlers came and for a time thereafter, most of this was good grassland. At points along the main streams there were villages of farming Indians—Caddo, Tonkawa, and some branches of the Wichita. But by about 1870 there were no Indians at all left along the Bosque, settled or mobile, except perhaps for a few sad, drunken hangers-on about the towns. The white men had it to themselves, to use for mixed farming and stock raising in a pattern that had been evolving on the Texas frontier and was both reminiscent of life in the woodlands east to the Atlantic and prophetic of life as it would be lived on the untimbered plains.

By JOHN GRAVES

Most plowed and planted and reaped—foodstuffs in the earliest days but later and increasingly cotton, that ancestral cash crop which proved adapted to the Grand Prairie's soils and rainfall. Probably they kept some chickens and bees and hogs in the old pattern and had fruit trees and a kitchen garden. Yeomen in ancestry and type, they did their own work or helped one another do it; hardly any had brought slaves. Their houses, in the days before pine lumber began coming in from East Texas, were likely to be made of post-oak logs, for logs were at hand and so was the old woodland aptitude in their use.

But most also were heirs to the complex, violent skills that Mexicans and South Texans had worked out for handling longhorn cattle. As often as not, farmers along the Bosque ran a few cows or a good many on the open range that included the whole region except for fenced-off croplands, until barbed wire came in the eighties. Some men did nothing else. The westward-shifting Chisholm Trail ran close by, carrying big South Texas herds northward and the wagons of settlers heading out for new country. Feeling the trail's tug, young men sometimes rode north with a herd to savor the joys of the Kansas railheads, maybe never to come back. Or maybe they did come back to raise cotton and cows, to help shape a town, to organize schools, to celebrate life at dances and weddings, to reinforce by their attendance one of the little new hard-shell churches which, far more than the skimpy apparatus of law enforcement, held that world at one remove from anarchy.

Iredell was building when Clara came along, its few hundred inhabitants abrim with the feel of destiny that little western towns had in those days, the expectation of boom and growth. Her father was one of its builders, a carpenter and millwright who put up cotton gins all around the region as that king crop extended its sway, and erected pleasant, stout, simple frame houses, among them one for his own family on a high bluff overlooking Iredell and the Bosque valley from the north, where his daughter grew up with a panoramic view of things. The pine he used for building was hauled in at first by ox or mule wagons and later by the railroad, that ultimate nineteenth-century symbol of destiny, whose arrival at her village Aunt Clara witnessed and has set down dynamically on canvas.

She has in fact set down most of the things that struck her strongly about that world, freezing its essences for us in a creative outpouring that began long after she had moved away from the Bosque to live in Dallas, after her children were grown, after her husband had died. She reached back into a phenomenal memory that includes events from a time when she could hardly walk ("It kind of leaves a picture; you just see it the way it was") and, encouraged at first by teachers who were mainly wise enough to let her work flow by itself, made painting after painting whose cumulative effect is a communication of the wholeness and innocence and excitement of village life along the Bosque, as seen by a bright child and young woman in the latter quarter of the last century and the early years of this one.

Two details from Aunt Clara's oil My Birthplace, *which she painted in 1966*

Somewhat in the manner of the garden dial that marks only sunny hours, Aunt Clara has nearly always painted pleasant things. She likes subjects, she has said, that are "pretty and true, but not sad." In her this is less a sentimental Victorian trait than a frontier female one, for with trouble and hardship and violence all around, if you let yourself dwell on them you stopped functioning; and functioning mattered.

Thus what we see in her paintings are matters for pride or joy—the hard, accepted work of the times with cows and crops and clothes and food; religion deeply and daily felt; play in the form of fishing and swimming and dancing and picnicking and other village pleasures; and special moments such as the big freeze, the arrival of the Texas Central, Christmas in the log house of her babyhood, even grown-up Clara's first fascinated glimpse of an airplane.

What we do not see are the darker, more masculine aspects of life along the Bosque, nor anything about the starkness and melancholy that gradually invaded the land as destiny moved on elsewhere, and dependence on an ever skimpier single cash crop put farmers at the mercy of faraway markets, and the soil of the fields thinned and gullied and blew away under such exploitative use, and over them and the once magnificent grasslands crept a blanket of cedar and scrub oak and mesquite.

One does not feel like carping about the lack. It can be filled in elsewhere, and Aunt Clara's omission of such things is not a denial of them. As an artist, she is a celebrant, and what she celebrates is the vigorous and high-hopeful spirit of the world that shaped her. Pretty and true, but not sad . . .

Iredell today, three quarters of a century and more after most of the events Clara Williamson has celebrated, dozes pleasantly beside the Bosque. Frontier vigor and high hopefulness, like destiny, departed long since, along with a good many of the people; for the town has shrunk to three or four hundred. The increasing proportion of elderly people are often retrospective—knowledgeable about the archaeology of old Iredell and about feuds and cemeteries and cattle trails, happy to talk with you on street corners and in cafés and along fencerows, about a time when destiny still strode along the Bosque.

The railroad quit running in the 1920's, and now even the tracks and ties have been removed. Since boom has never laid its garish crust over the remnants of the local past, you can still easily find places and buildings, and even trees, from Clara Williamson's paintings (the house her father built, where she grew up, still stands on the height north of town overlooking all below), but the village scene is faded, dusty somehow, without the shining, optimistic neatness and bustle her pictures show.

The ambient countryside is tired and faded and retrospective, too, in large part—brushy, eroded, depopulated, its once rich fields turned mainly into sorry pastures, its streams low or dry for much of the year, many of its old plank houses empty and held from collapse only by the staunchness of their limestone chimneys. There is much wildlife, but of small varieties except for deer, which prosper in the brush as do the Angora goats that make up much of the area's livestock where there are fences that will hold them. Destiny's boots, one discerns without much difficulty, tromped a bit hard around these parts.

Yet increasingly, here and there, a contrasting freshness meets the eye—a rolling grassy stretch of prairie free of brush, taut-fenced, dotted with fat cows and shady live oaks as it was in the old days, with green, terraced fields sowed to forage crops in the bottomlands, and on a hill neat houses and barns and corrals. Such restoration has been achieved through the use of big modern machinery that clears and reshapes the land, and its results stand in hopeful contrast not only to what started happening in that region at the tail end of destiny's reign but to the sickening, continuing ruin of much of our national landscape elsewhere as a result of boom and growth.

Nevertheless, as the traditionalists of Iredell can point out to you, this process is rough on what is left of the region's old way of living. Land reclamation is expensive and takes a good while to start paying dividends. Often, for economic results, it involves the consolidation of little homestead holdings into ranch-sized tracts. Bought out, old families move away, and that much more of the old frontier relationship to the land, and its lore, and its strength, moves away with them to be ground down to modern sameness in larger towns and cities.

But it is one of the special American sadnesses that the frontier way of life was, by its own vigor and appetite and techniques, foredoomed. And if there is among us still a nostalgia toward it, there is also much consolation in the fact that a few people like Clara McDonald Williamson, who knew it in its freshness, have managed to set down some truths about it that let us share their understanding.

Formerly on the faculty of Texas Christian University, Mr. Graves is now a free-lance writer with special interest in conservation and in local history. The editors are grateful to Donald and Margaret Vogel, the authors of Aunt Clara: The Paintings of Clara McDonald Williamson (*University of Texas Press, 1966*) *for help in preparing the accompanying picture portfolio.*

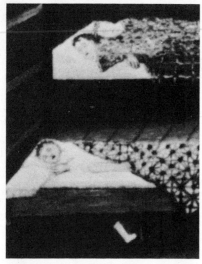

Details from The Night Before Christmas *evoke the holiday joys of a simpler era.*

he Building of the Railroad, 1949–50: COLLECTION OF MR. AND MRS. EDWARD DOUGLAS COBB, BARCELONA, SPAIN

It was a big day for Iredell when the railroad finally reached the town, and Aunt Clara never forgot it, though she was not yet quite five. Eighty years later she painted it all: the chuffing steam engine, the workmen laying ties and rails, the tents and chuck wagon at their camp site, a farmer's frightened team bolting and spilling his daughter out of the wagon, and the townspeople gathering to see the great sight. Clara is the child in blue in the foreground; her mother holds her baby sister in her arms. "I'm not afraid of that big iron thing," Clara recalls saying. Then the whistle blew, and her bravado vanished: "I was oh, so scared, and I grabbed Mama's skirt and hid."

49

Recess time at a country school is the subject of this pleasant painting, which like so many of Aunt Clara's catches her keen sense of the wide sky and lambent air of her part of Texas. The children play their games, horses browse, cool water is drawn from the well—and the teacher is poised with the bell.

The Girls Went Fishing *recalls one summer afternoon when three of Aunt Clara's friends blundered, with horrified fascination, upon a group of Iredell boys who were beating the heat with a dip in the Bosque River—naturally naked. Clara admits that she was already at the scene, peeking from behind a tree.*

When the weather was fine, even church services were held out of doors. Aunt Clara can name and tell a story about each member of the congregation shown here. Late arrivers are crossing the Bosque by "ferry"; the stepping stones, upriver, could be a bit treacherous when you had your Sunday shoes on.

A barn dance, in Aunt Clara's world, was an exciting social event. Children, awake or asleep, occupied the stalls; their parents stepped to the commands of the caller and the beat of country music; the young men looked over the nubile contingent in a more telling situation than, say, a prayer meeting.

The celebrated Chisholm Trail, along which millions of cattle were driven from the Texas range to railheads in Kansas, passed close by Iredell. As a small girl Aunt Clara often watched as they ambled by, and long afterward—after railroads and barbed wire had put an end to the drives—she painted out her memories in many cattle pictures. The Texas longhorns intrigued her especially, and she worked hard at improving her depiction of them. "When I look at some of my old pictures—well, I can find mistake after mistake," she once said of her early efforts on this theme. "The Old Chisholm Trail [above] is better. I really got the Texas longhorns right in that one."

The big cash crop around Iredell was cotton. Clara picked it herself in her youth, and among her memory paintings Cotton-Picking Time is one of the most effective compositions. (For once she enjoyed an easy triumph in her endless contest with perspective: the cotton rows helped out on that.) Behind them the workers trail their long, almost bottomless sacks as they pursue their tiresome work in the hot sun, although one has found a vagrant watermelon understandably irresistible. **Overleaf:** The Day the Bosque Froze Over commemorates a winter so cold that the town's weightiest citizens could and did walk on the river ice. The bridge made a splendid Euclidean backdrop.

A unt Clara left Iredell to live in Dallas, one hundred miles to the
northeast, shortly after the experience she recorded later in Transportation, the Old and the New, Circa 1919, Meridian,
Texas. *A friend invited her to motor down to Meridian to see the first airplane
ever to visit Bosque County. This was a double thrill for Clara: not only had she
never seen an airplane, but she had never been in an automobile. Her memory of the
plane may not be quite accurate—there were few high-winged monoplanes in 1919
—but the painting nicely evokes the excitement of the moment and the sense of a
rapidly shifting world, emphasized by the train chugging along in the distance.*

Aside from being the only private in Pancho Villa's army, my father had another distinction—he was probably the only man ever to be dragged into an army at the end of a harness. But, as any fair-minded person will concede, he was not trying to avoid military service; he was simply resisting an outrageous expropriation of his personal property.

His sudden "enlistment" occurred on a sultry October afternoon in the dusty little plaza of Bachimba, Chihuahua. My father had come to town to purchase a harness at Don Epifanio's general store, and many years later he could still recall the strange, ghostly silence that seemed to hover in every doorway as he entered the square. Only an occasional child greeted him when he clomped along the wooden sidewalk, half dragging an old cart with squeaky wheels. He was slightly more than seventeen years old.

He passed Don Miguel's barbershop, the old barber asleep in his swivel chair. This being the siesta hour, the three small stores beyond the barbershop-canteen were also closed and shuttered against the blistering sun. But Don Epifanio, a stay-awake *gachupín* from Madrid who was the only affluent merchant in that impoverished area, was predictably open for business when my father entered his store.

"*Qué tal, viejo,*" he said. (In Mexico people greet all boys as "old man" and all old men as "youngster.")

Emboldened by Don Epifanio's friendly familiarity, my father acknowledged the greeting and then inquired about the unusual quiet in Bachimba and the absence of any adults in the plaza.

"Then you have not heard?" asked the Spaniard. "Pancho Villa was here yesterday. With two hundred men he came. And he took ten sacks of flour from me, four jugs of tequila, and a dozen steel combs. Some other things, too. Then he told me to charge it."

My father glanced at the loaded shelves beyond the old man and wondered why Pancho Villa's men had left so much behind.

"And he also took some men with him," Don Epifanio added. "They grabbed Domingo Ortega, Jesus Silva, the Marquez boys, and that young man who helped me in the store. All of them are in the army now. That's why everybody's hiding now. That's why you don't see anybody in the plaza."

"But Villa's gone. You just told me."

"Not very far, *amigo*. He left a small cadre behind, just south of Bachimba. You can see their camp from the church tower. And you'd better get out of town, *muchacho*. Don Pancho may decide to draft *you* into his thieving army."

When my father mentioned that he was only seventeen, Don Epifanio knowingly observed that young boys, being more foolhardy and less circumspect than most adults, were probably preferred by the reckless vagabond leader of the fugitive *División del Norte*. But my father-to-be, having never seen that youthful army, had no basis for either agreeing or disagreeing with Don Epifanio's judgment nor for heeding his advice about getting out of town to avoid being kidnapped. He chose instead to dawdle, and the impatient storekeeper finally interrupted his browsing with an almost abrasive curt-

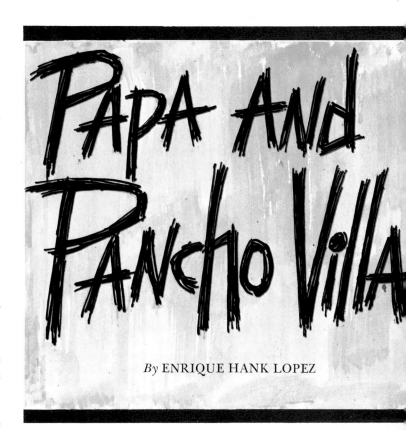

By ENRIQUE HANK LOPEZ

ness. "Surely you didn't come here to loaf. What do you want, boy?"

It was then that my father told him he might want to buy a new harness. But first he wanted to know if the old one (which he had hauled in the cart) could be repaired. It was ancient, its leather cracked and torn, and Don Epifanio scoffed at the possibility of salvaging it. With a heavy sigh of resignation my father tossed it into a waste barrel and proceeded to haggle about the price of a secondhand harness that the old man had reclaimed from a nonpaying customer from San Luis. My father (after two hours of sporadic bargaining) offered to pay seventeen pesos. Shortly before sunset they settled on a price of eighteen pesos and fifty cents, the old *gachupín* darkly muttering, "You're a worse bandit than Pancho Villa."

Modestly pleased by this minor triumph and no doubt flattered by the comparison to Villa, my father carefully stowed the harness in his cart and solemnly thanked Don Epifanio for a pleasant afternoon. The sun, by now a precise red-orange disk poised on the jagged silhouette of the barren sierra west of Bachimba, cast an amber glow on the deserted bandstand in the plaza as my father started to cross the street. Then quite suddenly a loud and probably drunken voice ordered him to halt. Four soldiers shuffled toward him in a crudely menacing manner.

"Where are you going, boy?"

"What do you have in that cart?"

The two voices rolled over each other, yet my father heard them both—clearly and separately. But before he could answer either question, one of the men reached for the newly bought harness. Instantly—his proprietary instincts overriding his fear—my father grabbed the harness and started to pull it toward him. With almost equal alacrity, the two soldiers snagged the halter and started pulling in the opposite direction. My father held on to the harness with mulish determination. They struggled for several minutes; then one of the soldiers gradually narrowed his emotions to plain unadulterated disgust.

"All right, you little bastard," he muttered, simultaneously reaching for his heavy pistol. "Since you're so in love with your lousy harness, you may as well stick with it. We're going to take you *both*, you and your harness, into the army." And that's exactly what they did. In one single act my father was both expropriated and drafted.

Ordinarily, one would have expected my father to continue his resistance and raise a bit of hell once he reached camp. He had, admittedly, a stubborn nature. But he calmly accepted his new status and was assigned the duty of stable hand in a cavalry unit, to which his harness had also been assigned.

The camp itself was a rather shabby affair consisting of three wind-battered tents stolen from a hacienda, a makeshift corral of seven horses, several sacks of flour piled on a flat-bed wagon, and—with my dad's arrival— twenty-nine soldiers, most of them younger than twenty. Their uniforms were the least uniform uniforms any army ever wore. No two men were dressed alike, although several of them wore the large, cumbersome, wide-brimmed sombreros that soon became the symbol of Villa's troops. However, whether in uniform or not, my father had no difficulty realizing that he was now a soldier. On the very first night he was handed a heavy rifle and ordered to serve as a lookout on a nearby hill.

"If you see any *federales chingados* just wake us up, and we'll get the hell out." Apparently this rear-guard cadre's sole responsibility was to shoot and run (in several different directions) and later regroup at a more southerly rendezvous.

Many years later, as we sat around the supper table in our rented flat in Denver, my father recalled in minute detail the awful fear that nearly paralyzed him as he stood guard on that scabrous hill four miles south of Bachimba. It was a quiet night, so deathly quiet that he could hear every lizard that skittered across the parched earth. And somewhere behind him—he was too frightened to ascertain its exact whereabouts—a lonely coyote moaned at fitful intervals. Yet his fear did not keep him from sitting down on a flat rock, where at last he fell sound asleep. He woke up at sunrise, stretched his cramped limbs until they felt normal again, and then walked slowly down the barranca toward the still-slumbering camp. "I'm a soldier now," he said to himself, a slight strut momentarily creeping into his gait. "I'm a private in Pancho Villa's army."

A few moments later he heard an abrupt snort from the tent nearest him, followed by a petulant grumbling that quickly crescendoed into a rolling thunder of curses that would have awed Satan himself. It was the capitan, Luis Jimenez, sounding reveille in his own piquant manner.

My father, who was no stranger to pungent language, forever claimed that Capitan Jimenez had the most violent, most profane, and most imaginatively obscene vocabulary he had ever heard. He had twenty-seven different expressions for homosexual, sixteen for unnatural birth, nine for canine maternal parentage, and a vast number of dark synonyms for murder and mayhem. Right now he wanted to get his detachment away from there.

Ten minutes later the tents were haphazardly folded and stashed next to the flour sacks on the flat-bed wagon, two horses were hitched to it with the previously expropriated harness, and they quickly pulled out of camp in a southerly direction. Having wisely decided not to ask permission to inform his parents about his spontaneous induction, my father rode in glum silence on the bumpy rear of the wagon. He wouldn't permit himself to cry, but his throat felt tight and bitterly dry.

Shortly before sunset, after long hours of tedium and discomfort, they finally caught up with the advance battalion. Pancho Villa himself greeted them as they shuffled into camp.

My father nearly gasped when he first saw Villa standing spread-legged by the huge bonfire, his voice booming a hearty "*Bienvenidos, muchachos.*" Here, then, was the legendary *Centauro del Norte* in the flesh! He was a big man by Mexican standards, with a head like a proud

lion and massive shoulders that strained the seams of his khaki tunic. But his eyes (not his large mustache, as most people think) were his most arresting feature.

"They seemed to burn with volcanic energy," my father later told us. "And yet there was a gentle mockery in those dark, intense eyes, a kind of teasing amusement that seemed to say there was nothing in the world that couldn't be laughed at." As for that famous mustache, which was to become a slobbery shank of messy hair in the movie portrayals by Wallace Beery and other actors, everyone who knew Villa insists that it was always clean and well clipped.

My father's first impression was a mixture of surprise and speechless awe. He was so dumbstruck by Villa's charismatic presence that he stumbled backward when the general moved forward to greet the new arrivals, bear-hugging two of the cadre leaders, shaking hands with some, and greeting others with friendly belly jabs, his rough, husky voice full of comradely warmth and cheerful obscenity. Then, suddenly noting my father shyly half hiding behind another soldier, he leaned out and grabbed my father's arm. "So this is one of our new comrades," he said. "What is your name, *muchacho?*"

"José Patricio Lopez Sepulveda." The name gushed from my father in a roll of frightened syllables.

"That's a large name for a small *muchacho*, but a good one."

"Everybody calls me Pepe," whispered my father. "Just Pepe."

"And where do you come from, Pepe?"

"From Bachimba—from Bachimba, Chihuahua—but we live on a rancho."

The smile of Villa's face broadened into a toothy grin. "Then you must know Martín Lopez—also from Bachimba."

"He's my cousin. Martín is my cousin." With less shyness now. "But he is much older. He's already twenty-five and I'm only seventeen."

59

"Ah, yes," answered Villa in his gently ironic manner. "Martín is getting to be an old man like the rest of us. But he's still young enough to raise hell with the *pinches federales*. He's one of my best men, Pepe, one of the toughest rebels in all Mexico."

Like everyone else in Bachimba, my father knew that Martín Lopez had once pulled a gun on Villa and that his act of defiance had, curiously enough, resulted in his being assigned to Villa's *los dorados*, that famed inner circle of "golden ones" who might be equated with a modern-day Mafia.

Perhaps sensing my father's private knowledge, Villa pressed his arm with a certain intimacy and quietly said, "Martín Lopez is the only man who ever openly defied me. And it takes much courage, Pepe, it takes *great* courage to defy Pancho Villa. Now he's one of my *dorados* and also a most trusted friend."

Martín Lopez rode into camp on the following afternoon, and shortly thereafter my father was summoned to Villa's command tent by a gruff, potbellied sergeant. When they finally reached the large officers' tent, Villa and another man were studying a map spread on the dirt floor, the noncom having to clear his throat twice to catch their attention. Villa looked up and quickly recognized my father. "Martín," he said, touching the other man's shoulder, "I have a surprise for you. Here's your little cousin Pepe."

"My God—it is! It's little Pepe, my little cousin Pepe." Martín grabbed my father and warmly embraced him, nearly squeezing him breathless. "But what are you doing here, *muchacho?*"

"He's our newest volunteer," said Villa. "We volunteered him three days ago. Near Bachimba."

"But he's only a boy, my general. He can't be more than sixteen," protested Martín. "The last time I saw him—about three years ago at my uncle's ranch—he was only thirteen years old."

Sensing an abrupt end to his military career, my father shook his head and stammered, "No, no, no, Cousin Martín! You're wrong—really you are—I'm seventeen—I'm already a man—I really am—I'm seventeen—and I want to stay."

"Don Pancho" (as many people called him with great affection) put his arms around the boy's slight shoulders and held him tight. "Perhaps your cousin is right, Pepe. Maybe you'd better go home. We may need you later on, *muchacho.*"

My father wheedled and cajoled and argued with desperate conviction, and finally, after an hour of futile polemics, they agreed to let him remain on condition that he serve as personal aide to Martín Lopez for the duration of the revolution. Thus, though he could not have anticipated it then, my father was soon to bear wit-

ness to some of the most exciting and daring exploits of that prolonged and bloody *revolución*, and his cousin was destined to become one of the most feared soldier-bandits in northern Mexico. Yet Martín Lopez was surprisingly gentle when my father panicked during his first exposure to gunfire. This happened late in November, 1913.

The federal troops had been harassing Villa's rear guard and were apparently planning a major advance along a railroad route north of Candelaria, in Sonora, where they had temporarily stopped to replenish themselves with food, women, and ammunition. Villa learned of their plans and fell back on one of his favorite tactics:

to immobilize the enemy by blowing up its troop trains before departure. This, of course, was always a rather tricky and suicidal maneuver requiring a special kind of talent and courage.

On this occasion Villa assigned the chore to Martín Lopez and Rodolfo Fierro, each of whom was to select five aides. Quite understandably, Martín bypassed "little Cousin Pepe" in choosing his five; but after several hours of spirited lobbying my father persuaded him that he could never become an experienced soldier unless he could have some experience. He thus became the thirteenth man in a sabotage team that was immediately dubbed the Odd Dozen.

Shortly after sunset the squadron pulled out of camp heading south, nine of them on horseback and four others walking alongside two large mules laden with dynamite. My father was one of the four on foot. They travelled several hours through pitch blackness, skirting the dirt highways and hugging the foothills, where an occasional cactus or bush offered at least minimal concealment from prospective enemy scouts. An hour before sunrise they sighted the troop train on a siding near the town of Candelaria. They could spot only one guard slouched against the rear platform of the caboose. "There are probably more guards on the other side," Martín whispered to Fierro. "But we have a fairly clear approach from this side."

After a brief second look he ordered the squadron to unpack the dynamite and divide it into packets of four sticks bound together with baling wire. Everyone having been given two packets and a pair of fuses, Martín drew a rough sketch of a railroad car, quickly explained his special demolition technique, and then assigned a car to each man. Fierro was to blow up the caboose and Martín the engine. With only a bare half hour of darkness remaining, the thirteen saboteurs fanned out in a wide arc and stealthily crept their way across the scrubby plain.

To his great surprise my father felt no fear during this phase of the operation. All he could think about was the fourth car behind the engine, its silhouette looming larger and larger as he got closer. Suddenly he was there, right under the middle of its "long belly" (Martín's term for it), and now he had to find the cross rod. His head bumped against it, and he was momentarily stunned. But he quickly regained his composure, pulled the dynamite packets from inside his shirt, tied them onto the cross rod, attached the fuse cord, and slowly commenced to unravel it while he crept backward in a crouched position. Glancing to his right he saw his *compañeros* also pulling back from their respective cars in crouched positions, with their fuse cords unravelling. Fierro had apparently stabbed the man guarding the caboose, so until now they had not been detected by the *federales*. It was like a well-rehearsed game.

Then, quite suddenly, the sky seemed to shatter. Someone had spotted Martín as he was crawling away from the engine and immediately shouted a general alarm. Almost instantly the air was punctured by a wild scattering of bullets, most of them whistling into nowhere. Taking advantage of the brief chaos, the Odd Dozen hastily ignited their fuses, carefully laid them on the ground, and started crawling away, zigzagging every few feet to avoid gunfire. Once again following Martín's lead, they commenced shooting back, hoping to distract attention from the sizzling fuses. Thus crawling and shooting and crawling once again, most of them managed to reach a safe distance before the railroad cars started to explode, first the engine and then the passenger cars, one after the other like falling dominoes. But the fourth car behind the engine—the one assigned to my father—did not explode. It merely teeter-tottered off the track as the cars on either side were blasted off the

rails. That's when my father, pausing to look back at the massive wreckage, remembered that in his panic he had forgotten to ignite his fuse.

When they finally got back to their horses and quickly mounted them for the getaway, it became painfully apparent that six of their *compañeros* had been killed or disabled. Although four of the thirteen saboteurs had come on foot, escorting the ammunition mules, there were now two extra horses. My father, still acutely conscious of having flubbed his chore, deliberately trailed behind the others as they raced toward the protective shadows of the Sierra Madre foothills. He was heartsick and depressed, and when they had found a safe haven he told his older cousin about the unlit fuse and about the only car that hadn't exploded, reluctantly but frankly admitting he had panicked as the gunfire broke out.

Martín looked at him with gentle cousinly concern and drew him into a tight embrace. "Never mind, Pepe, never mind. It happens to all of us. The man who says he's never afraid is a liar or a fool. Even Pancho Villa is afraid sometimes. He simply hides his fear better than most men. And you'll learn to hide yours, Pepe. It takes time."

During the next few months my father did indeed learn to mask or at least ignore the awful fear. He ostensibly overcame his qualms in a succession of historic battles late in 1913, the first of which took place in San Sostenes, Durango, where the *Villistas* attacked a federal-army supply center in a bold maneuver that caught the enemy flat-footed during the siesta hour. That particular raid, which turned into a spirited hand-to-hand ruckus before the *federales* retreated into the hills, netted the rebels two tons of clothing, several thousand rounds of ammunition, and some miscellaneous railroad equipment.

Two weeks later Martín Lopez led a band of fifty specially chosen guerrillas into the town of Mulato, Chihuahua, a wind-blown village temporarily designated as a headquarters for the forces of Venustiano Carranza, the leader of the Constitutionalists. Again relying on surprise plus outrageous daring, the rebels moved in shortly after midnight. Except for a few drunkenly inattentive guards, the federal troops had taken refuge in an old adobe church facing the plaza, the more fortunate ones lying on rows of wooden benches while the others shared the hard-packed dirt floor with an occasional scorpion. Having wenched and drunk pulque all evening long, they were sleeping quite soundly in spite of the hard bedding; and only two or three of them were even half awakened as Martín's men carefully crept over inert bodies and between the benches, deftly expropriating rifles, pistols, knives, and ammunition. Then, having first posted his men at strategic places inside the chapel—fourteen of them now armed with newly acquired machine guns—Martín asked his bugler to blow a rousing three o'clock reveille.

The ensuing blast, needless to say, was not too graciously received by the 260 bleary-eyed *federales*. They were even less gracious when ordered to remove their trousers and start marching toward the next town. Thirty rebels escorted them on horseback. Two hours later, as dawn broke over the ragged foothills, the rebel escorts abandoned the shivering, trouserless marchers on a long stretch of desert plain and galloped back to Mulato. They arrived in time for breakfast. Cheerfully attended by the grateful womenfolk of that impoverished but hospitable village, Martín's fifty men ate huge servings of tamales, *huevos rancheros*, hot *tortillas*, and *frijoles refritos*, after which they packed their looted rifles and ammunition on ten of the captured mules and headed back to Villa's headquarters in the city of Durango.

Shortly after their arrival there on January 1, 1914, Pancho Villa ordered Martín's men to join several other rebel contingents at Ojinaga, Chihuahua, where a large force of *Carranzistas* was heavily entrenched. This particular battle was the most disastrous event my father was ever to witness. Initially there were three days of furious fighting, the outnumbered rebels periodically picking and snapping at the well-fortified *federales* like packs of angry but toothless coyotes. Ojinaga was situated on a flat, barren desert that offered no chance of cover for an attacking group. Thus, in the absence of any clearly defined strategy, the rebels continued their fitful in-and-out forays, eighty men losing their lives in senseless assaults across wide-open areas murderously exposed to machine guns. Then an enemy cavalry unit closed in from the north in a lightning thrust that sandwiched 130 *Villistas* between two layers of firepower. Some of them tried to escape and were quickly shot down; the others prudently threw down their arms and surrendered. Brutally prodded with rifle butts, the prisoners were marched into the square and incarcerated in a local church. My father was among them, but somehow he managed to escape into a tiny corridor that led to a dark, narrow staircase winding up to the bell tower. There, alongside the belfry, he found a cracked and discarded bronze bell, and he snuggled into it like a frightened cat.

Long after nightfall (he never knew exactly when, for he had finally fallen asleep) he heard the staccato bark of machine guns somewhere beneath him, then a short silence followed by another brief volley, and then silence again. He simply could not imagine why anyone would be firing a machine gun inside a church, nor was he anxious to find out. Shifting his tired body into a reversed coil inside the bell, he soon managed to fall asleep again, and he was not fully awakened until just after dawn, when the dreamy silence was shattered by loud, angry voices from the plaza. He scrambled to his knees, shook the grogginess from his head, and then cautiously crawled across the roof toward the edge facing the square. Below him my father recognized some of the men from Martín's brigade. At first he thought they had been taken captive but then quickly noticed they were carrying arms. He bounded to his feet and raced across the roof and down the narrow stairs into the main chapel.

In his wild excitement he stumbled across two inert bodies before he realized that the floor was littered with bullet-shattered corpses, many of them grotesquely sprawled over each other in pools of drying blood. Some of the faces were mangled beyond recognition. Stunned and soon sickened by the horror all around him, he backed into the corridor, and there he felt a soft comforting hand on his shoulder. It was Cousin Martín, standing close to him with an unutterably sad expression in his eyes.

"How did you escape?" Martín asked in a near whisper. "I thought you were dead, Pepe. I was just now searching for your body. And then I saw you." My father slowly explained how he had sneaked up to the tower and slept through the awful massacre beneath him. Then Martín told him how the *federales*, apparently but erroneously assuming that Pancho Villa was sending a large battalion to reinforce his men at Ojinaga, had abandoned the town long before daybreak. But they had first of all murdered their 130 prisoners inside the chapel.

To my father the mass execution of Ojinaga would always represent the absolute depth of cruelty. And to Pancho Villa's men, particularly to *los dorados* like Martín, it would serve as justification for acts of equal depravity.

Yet no war is without its lighter aspects. One need not be a Hemingway to observe that between battles there might sometimes occur a moment of sexual whimsy. One such moment came to Pancho Villa late in 1915, when he fell in love with Conchita del Hierro. They had met in Jiménez, Chihuahua, through the auspices of her Aunt Clotilda, a person with no discernible excess of modesty. She was, in fact, an ambitious bawd, and within three days after the *División del Norte* had moved out of Jiménez she sent the general a note by personal messenger telling him that her niece had been greatly impressed with his "gentility" and was most anxious to see him again. His response was characteristically immediate and expansive. Summoning Martín to his headquarters tent—they were now in Guadalupe, Zacatecas—he asked him to go forthwith to Jiménez and bring back Conchita and her aunt.

"Take an engine and a caboose and enough men to run them," he said. "Treat them with all consideration, Martín. Their every wish must be granted." Then, with a vaguely skeptical glance at his much younger and more handsome comrade, he added, "And don't forget that Conchita is *my* girl. No monkey business, *amigo.*"

Early that afternoon Martín and five *compañeros* chugged out of the railroad station, my father stoking the boiler of the engine and doubling as assistant porter. He was in high good spirits all the way to Jiménez, whistling "Adelita" over and over again, periodically scraping the coal shovel as accompaniment—but his spirits soared even higher when he first saw Conchita.

Her shy, tentative smile and soft voice made the men feel that she was altogether unaware of her exquisite mestizo face and lithe, slender body. On the assumption that Villa would find the girl more desirable if her shoulders were half exposed, her aunt had forced her to wear a skimpy lace blouse, but Conchita had nullified this erotic ploy by wearing a thick black *rebozo* that shielded her like a nun's cape. Indeed, as she got off the caboose at Guadalupe, her entire demeanor was that of a young nun, her frightened eyes glinting now and then with helpless resentment, her naturally full lips pulled into a tight, childlike pout.

Villa, waiting on the platform to greet them, instantly realized that Aunt Clotilda had lied to him about the girl's yearning desire to see him again; yet his ego was not prepared to admit what his eyes clearly told him. "*Bienvenidos!*" he said with determined gusto. "I was beginning to think Martín had kidnapped you."

Not to be outdone by the general's effusiveness, Aunt Clotilda, pushing the reluctant girl forward, also gushed with good cheer. "She's here, Don Pancho. You see I've kept my word. But the child's overcome with fatigue and excitement. We'll have to rest a while."

"Yes, yes, of course. That's a long journey."

Briskly assigning four aides to escort the ladies to a small hacienda nearby, Villa almost recovered his composure in the process of snapping orders. But not quite. His men, at least those close to him, could see that Conchita's manner had deeply shaken him. And during the next forty-eight hours she managed—not with malice, nor even by the slightest intention—to bruise his pride as few women would have dared. She locked herself in the master bedroom, pushed a heavy divan against the door, and simply refused to see either Villa or her aunt.

In the end Conchita had her way. My father was far from surprised when the girl and her aunt abruptly left the hacienda on Friday morning, riding a plain buckboard wagon in considerably less grandeur than upon their arrival. While helping them with their luggage he heard the enraged aunt scolding her niece.

"You foolish child," she said bitterly. "That man will be president of Mexico, and you could be the first lady."

Several months later Pancho Villa's troops marched into Mexico City, and he temporarily seized the national palace, proclaiming himself president. Had she been more expedient, Conchita del Hierro would have been first lady for seventy-two hours. She might have also been shoved aside by the fickle *Centauro del Norte*, for he was notoriously inclined to break his word. On several occasions, for example, he promised to promote my father to corporal—one of the many promises he never kept.

José Patricio Lopez Sepulveda remained a lowly private for three long years, after which he fled across the border to El Paso, Texas, to escape the ultimately triumphant

federales. As a child living in a Mexican neighborhood in Denver, where everyone's father bragged about having been officers and noncoms, I was never fully reconciled to his unique status as the only private in that famous rebel army. I, in fact, sorely resented Pancho Villa for failing to promote him. Not until recently have I come to appreciate the ironic whimsy that no doubt prompted my father's quiet refusal to elevate himself to an officer's rank.

I now have the suspicion that he was really a full corporal.

Enrique Hank Lopez, a New York lawyer and free-lance writer, bridges two cultures in his articles for this magazine. Recently he was the editor of Sam Houston Johnson's amusing and intimate biography, My Brother Lyndon *(Cowles, 1970).*

A Mission for Mr. Wedgwood

The distance between Charleston, South Carolina, and Franklin, North Carolina, is just about three hundred miles—a comfortable day's drive over well-paved, scenic highways. For Thomas Griffiths the journey was a good deal more arduous, and it took him a good deal longer to accomplish, particularly since he didn't really know where he was going.

Thomas Griffiths was the brother of Ralph Griffiths, editor of the Monthly Review, *a popular periodical in England in the middle eighteenth century. Ralph Griffiths, in turn, was a friend of Josiah Wedgwood (1730–1795), the great English potter. Wedgwood's success as a manufacturer during the Industrial Revolution was due to many factors, not least to his ardent passion for improving his product by constant research and invention—the carrying out of a lifetime of experimentation not only in seeking new raw materials but also in mixing them in different proportions and firing them under different conditions of temperature and atmosphere.*

JOSIAH WEDGWOOD & SONS. LTD. BARLASTON. STOKE-ON-TRENT

A classic example of Wedgwood art —a jasper vase modelled in 1784

ment to block such a monopoly. The wisest thing, the Duke felt, was for Wedgwood to find someone who knew the American colonies and might act as his agent. The ideal man for this assignment turned up in the person of Thomas Griffiths. To Bentley, Wedgwood wrote: "Our friend Mr. [Ralph] Griffiths has a Bro. who hath resided many years in N.A., & is seasoned to the S.C. climate by a severe fever he underwent at Chas. Town & has had many connections with the Indians. He had been a Proprietor of 3,000 acres near Crown point . . ." Griffiths gamely accepted Wedgwood's challenge.

Like most travellers and tourists of that era Griffiths kept a journal during his mission. It is so full of adventure and so descriptive of the topography of the country and of the customs and mores of the population, colonists and Indians alike, that a major portion of it is published here, with Griffiths' original spelling and grammar.
—H. C. W.

In his search for new minerals, earths, and clays Wedgwood had his friends send him samples of likely materials from all over the world, including the American colonies. Sometime during the year 1766–67, one of his friends, a Mr. Vigor of Manchester, sent him a sample of white Cherokee clay, or "steatites," which the Indians in South Carolina reputedly used to make their pipes.

With his customary energy Wedgwood set about to get all the information he could. To his partner Thomas Bentley he wrote in May, 1767: "I am in search of the Town where the Steatites grows, & I believe I shall learn every particular about it. One Dr. Mitchell has just published a map of N.A. which map I have purchased . . . I find the Town in his Map to be Ayoree, & . . . I am pretty certain it is the place."

The location established, the question remained as to how to go about obtaining a bulk sample. Wedgwood's friend and patron Francis Egerton, third Duke of Bridgwater, advised him not to apply to the Parliamentary Lords of Trades and Plantations for a sole franchise to import the clay because his competitors would hear about it and bring pressure on their members of Parlia-

London July ye 16—went on board the Ship America Capt. Raineer Comd, & bound to Chas. Town & . . . [we arrived] in Chas. Town Bay on the Twentyfirst of September, being a Miserable hot and Sickly time.

In this Port I remain, till Sunday the fourth of October, and then went off for the Cherokee Nation: The first stage was Dorchester, Twenty five Miles from Charles Town: from thence to Beakons Bridg, then over the Cypress and four holes, being very deep and daingerous Roads, and exceeding Trublesome for Straingers: Then on to Walnuttree Creek and Parish end, fifty miles from Charles Town; here I saw the people Reaping fine Rice; the next stage was Capt Wm. Youngs; This is a middling good Tavern and a fine Rice plant[at]ion:

The weather was now very hot and fainty, and the people allmost all dying of the ague and feaver; here my horse fell lame which obligd me to send my Baggage by a Waggon, and also to Make very short Stages;

Introduction and Epilogue by HENSLEIGH C. WEDGWOOD

the next place I came to, was Oringburg, which is a Considerable Large Neighbourhood, and afoards a Tavern, a Shop or Storekeeper and a Man that pretended to Preach; here my horse obliged me to stop two nights, and then Proceeded for Indian head; and after a hot days March was obliged to sleep under a Tree with my horse, very near the place where five people had been Robd and Murdered but two days before, by the Virgina Crackers and Rebells; a Sett of Thieves that were joind together to Rob Travillers and plunder and destroy the poar defenseless Inhabitants of the New Settlements—

The next day I went on for a place calld the Ridge, in this days journey I very Luckily joind company with a Trader, a thing very rare to see either Person or so much as a poar hutt for Twenty or Thirty Miles ride thro these woods; after we had Travild about six miles, and near sun sett, he told me he saw two fellows ahead that he did not very well Like, and prayd me to give him one of my Pistolls and keep the other in my hand ready cockd; and as my new companion expected, they soon gallopd up a Deer Track into our Road, with a "how do you do Gentlemen, how farr have you cum this Road? have you met any horse men?," and then wishd us a good evening; but soon stoppd and asked if we had heard any News about the Robers, which we answered in the nagative & so on: my Companion then said, it was well we were together, and that we had fire arms, as he had some knowledge of one fellow and believed him to be concernd in the late Murder, which proved too true; as he was took in a few days after, and I saw him Executed at Chas.Town in february following:

By this time we were very near a place calld the Ridge, a small pleasant village and a Tavern, but frequently Visited by Thieves; here my fellow Traviler wishd me good night, but advised me only to refresh my Self and horse and not sleep there, Lest I might chance to want a horse next Morning, and perhaps that not the worst of it: I took my friends advice, and went five miles further and lay in the wood: but this proved not very lucky, as my Beast happened to break his hobble and stray a great way from me, which obligd me to hunt him for severall hours with the Sadle on my back; and it being a very dewy Morning, gave me a great Cold and much disordered me;

The next day I proceeded for Coffee Creek, a new neighbourhood lately inhabited near the Kings Road . . . the next day I Marchd on for Andrew Williamsons at White hall near a place calld hard Labour, about two hundred miles from Charles Town:

This is one of the finest plantations in South Carolina; abounding with fine Rich Red Loomy Land, famous for raising corn, hemp, flax, Cotton, Rice, Cattle, Hogs, fruits of all sort, and great plenty of Mulberries, white

& black Gooseberries excepted; but Peachs inumerable: friend Williamson said, in the year Sixty Six his peach orchard yielded near Three Thousan Bushel Baskets; which proved of great use to the poar young inhabitants of that part of the province; besides feeding him a great number of hogs &c. . .

On the Seventeenth of October I left this place in Consort with an Indian Woman belonging to the Chiefs of the Cherokees, who had been long stole away by the Youghtanous, and afterwards Ransomd by our Indian deputy of the Illinois . . . on the Eighteenth we came to Capt. Aron Smiths; at this Tavern we found midling good Beds, but were obligd to sleep in the woods the two preceeding nights; and on the Twentieth we arrived at Fort Prince George calld old Keowee; which is the first settlement in the Nation, and about forty Miles from the Indian Line calld Jewetts corner:

At this Fort I deliverd up my Squaw and Letters to Ensign McKeough, the commanding officer of that place; who recd me with much politeness: here also I met with Capt. Cameron our deputy Commissary for Indian affairs; and likewise the great Prince of Chotee, . . . [and] most of the Chiefs of the Cherokee Nation;

All then, met at this Fort to call a Counsell and hold a grand Talk concerning a peace with the Norward Enemies; and to apoint proper persons to proceed to New York and the Mohawk Nation, for that purpose; after I had Eat, drank, Smokd and began to be familier with these Strainge Copper Collourd Gentry, I thought it a fair opportunity to request Leave to Travill through their Nation, in Search [of] anything that curiosity might lead me to; and in particular to Speculate on their Ayoree white Earth; and accordingly the Commanding Officer made the Motion, and the Linguist was desired to be very particular on the subject: This they granted, after a long hesitation, and severall debates among themselves; the Young Warier, gone more, seem'd to consent with some reluctance; Saying, they had been Troubled with some young Men long before, who made great holes in their Land, took away their fine White Clay, and gave 'em only Promises for it: however as I came from their father and had behaved like a true Brother in taking care to conduct their Squaw safe home, they did not care to disapoint me for that time; but if I shod want more for the future, they must have some satisfaction; for they did not know what use that Mountain might be to them, or their Children; and if it would make fine punch Bowls, as they had been told, they hopd I wod let em drink out of one; and thus we Shoke hands and settled the matter . . .

At this place there runs a fine Valley between the hills a Considerable way down the Savanah River, and exceeding fine rich land; but I had not the pleasure to enjoy much of it, as at that time, it was very daingerous to go from the reach of the Fort guns; however on Sunday the Twentyfifth, I venturd to ride so far as Keowee new Town, and Sugar Town, which is about four Miles from the Fort; but I must own I was a little in fear of every Leaf that rattled: at these Towns I saw but few Indians for they were all gone out a hunting, excepting the old Squaws and young naked Vipers; besides a few old beloved Men and Conjurers, who Behaved with some Civility and gathered me fine Grapes and May Aples: here likewise I visited my old Consort the Queen, who acording to the Indian Custom, was obligd to undergoe Eight days of Confinement in the Town house, after returning from, or being a Prisoner to any Enemy whatsoever, and after that to be Stripd, dipd, well washd and Conducted home to their Husband, wife or friends. . .

On the Thirtyeth of October I took leave of this Fort, and proceeded for the Middle Settlement and Mountains, Crossing the Chattoga River at the Warwomans Creek; allso the Six deviders, besides a great Number of small Brooks and fine springs that have their Course between the Mountains; but the Savanahs are in some places very Rotten and daingerous for Strange Travillers; in severall parts a Man and his horse may sink in fifteen or Twenty foot and must unavoidable perish . . . it was then the Miserablist weather I ever was exposed too; haveing the Wind strong at N.E. with Cold and heavy rain or sleet, from five in the morning, till nine at night; when I arrived at an Indian hutt which was the first shelter I could cum at; and by that time there was scarce Life in me or my poar horse; and when I advanced near the fire, it overcame me and I fell down: and unluckily the Master was gon out, so that I had no other refreshment than Potatoes bread & Water and Indian Corn for my horse; but the poar Squaw dryed my Cloaths as well as she could and wrapd me in a Blanket and Bear Skin, and the next Morning Mr. Downy came home, for that was my Landlords name, who stewed me some Fowls, which made me a glorious Repast:

This being Sunday the first of November I set off for Patrick Gallihorn, at [illegible] Town on the Tenassee River, which runs into the Massisipy, and is five Miles from the Ayoree Mountain: here I remaind a few days, and furnished my self with a Servant, Tools, Blankets and Bear Skins; and on the Third of november we retired to the ayoree Mountain, where we remaind 'till the Twentythird of decemr;

Here we labourd hard for 3 days in Clearing away the rubish out of the old pitt, which could not be less than Twelve or fifteen Ton; but on the fourth day, when the pitt was well cleand out, and the Clay appeard fine; to my great surprise, the Chief Men of Ayoree came and Took me prisoner, telling me I was a Tresspaser on their land and that they had recd instructions from Fort George, not to suffer their pitt to be opened on any account; and as to any consent of the head men of the Nation, they minded not, nor would they let any clay be dug under five hundred weight of Leather for every Ton: they also showd me a string of white Beads that the Young Warier had brought from the fort, as a firm Token of a faithfull and True Talk—This was a Mistake of some of the Gentle'n at fort George, which confounded me greatly, and I never yet had it cleard up; and have great reason to think there was some deceipt at the bottom; and proved of very ill Consequence to me, as it made the Indians set a high Value on their white Earth: however I sent for a Linguist and after a Strong Talk which lasted near four hours, we settld matters on such conditions, as I might obtain what I wanted without any further Molestation . . .

In four days from this, I had a Ton of fine clay ready for the pack horses, when very unfortunately the weather chainged, and such heavy rains fell in the night, that a perfect Torent flowd from the uper Mountains with such rapidity, that not only filld my pitt, but meltd, staind and spoild near all I had dug and even beat thro our wigwam and put out our fire, so that we were nearly perished with wet and cold: this weather provd of bad consequence another way, as it washed the Stratums of red earth that run Skirting thro the pitt, which staind and spoild a vast deal of white clay.

I have nothing more materiall to mention dureing the whole process of this work: the Indians were often paying me troublesome visits, indeed they would sometimes bring me a Little provision for good pay, and would often steal Trifles from me: however I Invited 'em Together and heated 'em with rum and such Musick as I was capable of, which made 'em dance with great agility, especially when the Bottle had gon about well; which is the only way to make friendship with any Indians, provided they are not made drunk: by this means matters went on very smooth between us, and they held me fast by the hand, Crowning and calling me great George's Warier &c; the old beloved man allso consented I shod have his best Bow and case of arrows, and also the old Princes pipe and Town house sanktion. Thus we continued and parted very good friends, but withall, they hoped I shod want but a few horse Loads of white clay, and prayd I would not forget the promise I made 'em, but perform it so soon as possible

On the Eighteenth of December I had dug & dryd all the clay I intended to take, and as the pack horses were then at the fort I had a few days to hunt, fossil & Botanise which I improved as much as possible, but I found many things very short of my expectation; I had allmost forgot to aquaint the Reader, what a severe winter it proved in this part of the world; the River Tenassee tho shallow at this place, and a strong current yet twice I saw it frozen over in the Mornings and the pott ready to freeze on a slow fire . . . I was never more sensible of the Cold . . .

On the Twentythird of Decemr I took Leave of this cold and Mountainous Country, and went off with the pack horses for fort prince George; but the Frosty Weather breaking, and the mountain paths being very narrow and Slipery, we killd and spoild some of the best horses; and at last my own Slipt down and roled severall times over me; but I saved my self by laying hold of a young tree, and the poar Beast Tumbled into a Creek & was spoild: This was an unlucky Sircumstance, as I had then severall hundred Miles to Travill . . .

On the Twenty Seventh, I arrived once more at Fort George, which believe me, was, at that time a wellcome prospect; and when I came up to the parade I could gladly have kissed the Soldiers for Joy:

Nothing of Moment occurd dureing my stay here, till January the fourteenth when I loaded five Waggons with Five Ton of Clay and set off for Chas.Town; but light horse, bad roads, and sollid Loading, obligd us to Travill very Slow: on the Eighteenth I lay with Parson Hamerer at Little River, then to Capt. Aron Smith's Tavern, and so on to Matthew Edward's, at Long Cane and the next day to Whitehall, where I waited four days for the Waggons: and then on to Coffee Creek, and lodged in the woods, and the next night allso at Turkey Creek: on the Twenty Seventh I came to the Ridge, where I stayed two nights, and so on to Indian head, where I slept again in the woods, and happening a very heavy Night's rain, gave me a great Cold and much disordered me; the next day's march brot me to Oringburg and the next day to Capt Wm Young's Tavern, and so on to the four holes

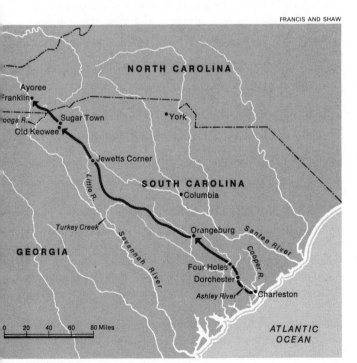

FRANCIS AND SHAW

A simple map of Griffiths' trip makes it look easy. It wasn't.

Hensleigh C. Wedgwood retired in 1958 from the world-famous pottery that was founded in 1759 by his great-great-great-great grandfather, who sent Thomas Griffiths to America. Mr. Wedgwood, now a resident of New York City, owns the original journal.

and Cypress; the next day to Dorchester, and on the fourth of february I arrived once more at dear, and long wishd for, Charles Town—

Nothing Materiall happened dureing my stay in this Capital; I saw severall Thieves executed that were Lurking about in the Woods I had Travilld thro, after this I saw a farr pleasanter sight, which was some very good horse Raceing, when we consider boath breed and Country young: This is a very gay and compact Town, finely situated on a peninsula, between Ashley and Cooper Rivers; and an exceeding good harbour for Shiping; here is boath good religion & Salutary Laws; and their divine Service is performd with great order and regularity: The people are mostly True Patriots and dear Lovers of Liberty; a great many of 'em carefull and thrifty; severall Eminent Merchants who Transact their Business very quick and discreet, but withall, there reigns too great a spirit of gaming amongst 'em, and they are arrived to a great highth of pride; they sertainly do, and can afoard to live very well, as provision is boath plenty and cheap, but in truth they take care to make Straingers and Travilling people pay dear enough—

On the first of March I agreed for Freight and passage with Capt. Morgan Griffiths of the Rialto, Bound for London; and on the fourth we bid farewell to Chas. Town . . .

April the first we spoak the John and Ann Brig bound from London to Newfound Land in Latt 48-46W. Long 17-40 and on the fourteenth of Aprill we arrived in the Downs; and the Sixteenth Capt. Griffiths, Mr John Smith and my self Left the Ship in the Pilots charge at Graves End and came to London by Land.

Thus the great adventure was ended, and in due course the Cherokee clay reached its final destination. Considering the fact that its cost worked out at about £130 per ton, which was a considerable sum of money in those days, and the fact that the mining of white clays of equal or superior quality had been developed in Cornwall, it was a highly uneconomic proposition. But this didn't faze Wedgwood one bit. "It might not be a bad idea," he wrote to Bentley, "to give out that our Jaspers are made of the Cherokee clay which I sent an agent into that country on purpose to procure for me, & when this present parcel is out we have no hopes of obtaining more."

There is no moral to this story, but it does reveal the extraordinary pioneering zeal that, indirectly, was so largely responsible for the Industrial Revolution and that characterized those hardy colonists who braved the elements and the Indians to open up a new country.

A Clean Break...

CONTINUED FROM PAGE 7

and a listing of some of them gives a remarkable picture of the preoccupations of the time: *atomic cloud, be-bop, buyers' strike, existentialism, fact finder* (as in a labor dispute), *fissionable, gray market, iron curtain, operation* (as in Operation This-or-That), *push-button* (as a metaphorical adjective), *shock wave, sitter* (for babysitter), *truth serum, U.N., UNESCO.*

Fact finder, fissionable, sitter: talismans of the time, casting strange shafts of light into the future. It was a time of getting settled. That, of course, meant more than veterans coming home; it also meant industrial workers demanding the raises that had been deferred by wartime controls, and therefore strikes. In November, 1945, there began a series of crippling strikes in key industries. Meanwhile, as the government vacillated on price controls, meat disappeared from grocery shelves for days at a time because of speculative withholding by suppliers. None of these inconveniences held back the business of nest building. The year 1946 stands out as the all-time record year for marriages in the nation's history, not only relative to population but in absolute numbers—2,291,000 marriages all told, or almost 700,000 more than in 1945, and almost twice as many as there had been in the deep Depression years before the war. The first nest in 1946 was usually an apartment rather than a house; material shortages held up the beginning of the great postwar home-building boom, but even so, construction of one-family dwellings tripled between 1945 and 1946. And whatever their nature, the new nests were quickly fruitful. The national birth rate went up 20 per cent in 1946 over 1945 (that November, New York City actually ran out of birth certificates) and another 10 per cent in 1947 over 1946, as the celebrated postwar baby boom got under way.

So the ex-serviceman, in college on the GI Bill, with his pregnant wife struggling to make a palatable dinner on short meat rations in their barracks apartment, was earnestly trying to sop up the knowledge that would get him a civilian job, with no thought farther from his mind than questioning, much less protesting against, the social framework or the institution in which he worked. Nest-building time is not a time for rebellion. Also in 1946 the government was paring back its budget from 1945's one hundred billion to sixty billion dollars, and the next year it would spend less than forty billion; the infant United Nations was trying out its unsteady legs at the optimistically named Lake Success on Long Island; there were four lynchings in the South; the Bikini bomb tests were appalling us, and the Cold War was taking shape; radio was still the great national diversion, with Jack Benny first in the Hooperatings, Fibber McGee and Molly second, and—incredible as it now seems—Amos 'n Andy seventh. And while all these quaint happenings were in process, the word *existentialism* was coming into the American language.

Of such was the nest-building mood, the nation's first in the postwar period. There have been five more since then that I can distinguish: the Korean-war mood, the McCarthy mood, the Eisenhower-prosperity mood, the Kennedy go-go mood, and finally the present one of paralysis, gloom, and reappraisal.

Beginning with the North Korean invasion of South Korea on June 25, 1950, the Korean war was a time of nightmare. There was a kind of *déjà vu* about finding ourselves again embroiled in a war when we had just settled down to peace, and for thousands of veterans of the Second World War who had signed up for the reserves without thinking twice about it (I remember, for example, that when I was separated from the Army at Fort Dix, New Jersey, in 1945, they encouraged reserve enlistment by letting you out one day sooner if you signed up), it meant an actual return to combat. It was a new kind of war—not even officially called a war, but rather a "police action"—as frustrating as an unpleasant dream, that we could not win and apparently were not *supposed* to win. (We would learn more about that kind of war later.) The rumors we heard, later confirmed, that American prisoners were being subjected to a new and horrifying form of mental torture called brainwashing were literally the stuff of nightmare. So was the vision of an endless mass of humanity, bent on killing and seemingly unconcerned about being killed, that was embodied in the phrase "human wave," used to describe the Chinese Communist hordes that streamed south across the Yalu River in November, 1950. Finally, during the two years that the armistice talks dragged on at Panmunjom while the shooting continued, there was the nightmare sense of trying to wake up to a pleasanter reality and being unable to do so.

Shaken but relieved, the country finally awoke with the signing of the armistice on July 27, 1953—but awoke merely, as sometimes happens, from one level of nightmare to another. The time of the paid informer and the false witness had already come. As early as 1948 Whittaker Chambers had first made his charges of Communist spying against Alger Hiss, the apparently exemplary young statesman who had been a framer of the United Nations charter, and the Dreyfus case of modern America was launched. In 1949 eleven leaders of the U.S. Communist Party had been sent to prison; the following year Judith Coplon and Dr. Klaus Fuchs had been convicted of spying, the latter with reference to vital atomic secrets, and the young Senator Joseph McCarthy, seeing his chance, had made his famous series of accusations that there were 205 (or 57 or 81 or 10 or 116) Communists in the State Department. With that, the hounds of fear and distrust slipped their leashes, and by the time of the Korean armistice Senator McCarthy had made the nightmarishly irrational term "Fifth Amendment Communist" into a household expression; hardly any professional in the country could feel his job or his way of life safe from the random malice of almost anyone, and constitutional guarantees against just this sort of mischief were becoming all but meaningless.

That nightmare almost drove us crazy—perhaps came closer than we care to admit, even now. But finally our underlying national health asserted itself, and we awoke at last, this time definitively, in December, 1954, when the Senate censured McCarthy and McCarthyism went into decline. Small wonder, after such horrors, that the next mood should have been a recessive one, one of huddling in our shells and comforting ourselves with material things while remaining heedless of the mess we were making. The essence of the Eisenhower mood was long-deferred self-indulgence. It was a time of soaring stock-market prices and soaring participation in the boodle. The members of the middle class, the hugely expanding group that dominated the country, were becoming capitalists at last and were doing very well at it. It was a time of rocketing corporate profits and resulting fat dividends —at the cost of inflation and polluted air and water. It was a time of greatly increased leisure for millions—at the cost of littered roadsides and tamed and uglified national parks and forests. It was a time of more and more automobiles for more and more people—at the cost of traffic jams, more air pollution, eyesore automobile graveyards, and neglected public transportation. It was a time of bursting cities and proliferating suburbs—at the cost of increasingly neglected slums full of explosive anger quietly ticking away. It was a time when we thought of our "race problem" as being mainly a political matter confined to the South; when, in foreign policy, we fatalistically hid behind the dangerously provocative shield of "massive retaliation" and "brinkmanship" (and meanwhile were sowing the seeds of our Asian disaster); when college students kept a low profile, politically and otherwise, so as not to jeopardize their chances of flowing smoothly onto the production line to affluence right after graduation; and when—not so paradoxically as it may seem at first glance—the federal budget grew year by year and social security and other public benefits were greatly widened. The Eisenhower era is not to be compared too closely to that of Coolidge in terms of free enterprise's running wild. In the earlier

time the country had been all too truly committed to unrestricted free enterprise, but by the late fifties, despite Fourth of July paeans to the "American system" as fulsome as ever, the notion of cradle-to-grave security *for most people* had been thoroughly accepted and, indeed, assimilated into the system. The mood was heedless hedonism.

Next, in abrupt reaction, came the Kennedy years with their quite opposite mood of responsibility and hope. It is tempting now to think of those years as a golden age, though if we look closely we find they were scarcely that in practical terms; after all, Kennedy's domestic legislative defeats—on civil rights, on tax reform, on Medicare—far outweighed his victories, and he died leaving unsolved most of the problems he had inherited, including, of course, Vietnam. But his successful conclusion of the 1962 Cuban missile crisis, along with the limited nuclear test-ban treaty that followed the next summer, did much to allay the fear of nuclear war that had overhung the country all through the postwar period up to then. Much more important, he and his administration, through the almost magically inspiring quality of their very style, succeeded in regenerating the old American faith, not in the perfection of man or his nation but in their perfectability. No one despaired under Kennedy; somehow everything seemed possible. "I have a dream that one day this nation will rise up, [and] live out the true meaning of its creed . . ." Martin Luther King, Jr., said at the interracial March on Washington in August, 1963—a fitting epitome of the Kennedy mood, in a climax that no one could know came near the end of the last act.

Then everything went wrong. With Kennedy's death that November began an age of assassination; within five years probably the two most admired black men in the country, King and Malcolm X, and almost certainly the most admired white man, John Kennedy's brother Robert, would be dead from the same horrifying and dispiriting cause. During the same period more and more Negro leaders turned against King's dream, rejecting the American creed for a cynical, angry separatism; the hopeless war in Vietnam was escalated, and revelations about its conduct led many Americans to a similarly escalating sense of horror, disillusion, and shame; political colloquy at home became violent rather than reasonable; Americans achieved the technical masterwork of flying to the moon and back while failing to accomplish the technically simple one of giving all their citizens proper food and clothing. The sixth postwar mood was, and is, one of violence, disillusion, and doubt verging on despair such as has not been felt since the time of the Civil War.

It is my thesis, then, that while material change has generally been steady, continuous, and for the most part beneficent over the postwar period, the past five years or so have seen an explosive—and morally equivocal—increase in the rate of change in values and attitudes. It is in these last five years that most of our moral history since V-J Day has been written, and it is since 1965 that many Americans have come to feel like expatriates in America. In support of the thesis, let me tick off a few current American attitudes—now accepted widely enough among the influential, especially in the communications media, to constitute what might be called leadership opinion, if not national consensus—that would have been unthinkable not only on V-J Day but on the day of John Kennedy's death as well.

The attitude toward military affairs, and in particular toward our own military, has to a large extent undergone a reversal. My own generation, the one whose coming of age coincided with U.S. entry into the Second World War, had thought itself pacifist; we had been brought up on Dos Passos' *Three Soldiers* and Hemingway's *A Farewell to Arms* and the Nye investigation with its implication that wars are fought for the profits of munitions makers. But it turned out that our pacifism was only skin-deep; when the call to arms came, it found us full of sanguine enthusiasm. We wanted to be in it, and quickly, and we hurried to the recruiting offices; we thought of draft-dodging as contemptible and conscientious objection as respectable but, to say the least, highly eccentric. After Pearl Harbor a uniform, even that of an ordinary soldier or sailor, was a clear-cut asset in the pursuit of girls.

In the postwar period up until recently a uniform was neutral, considered neither glamorous nor unappealing. Not so now. There are no American "heroes" of Vietnam (not that there has been no actual heroism), and the sporadic efforts of the military to create some have failed utterly. On the contrary, among the heroes to today's youth, or a significant segment of it, are the evaders who are hiding out illegally in Canada or Sweden. Idealistic young people casually and openly discuss and choose among the legal and illegal ways of avoiding induction, and many of them consider the act of draft avoidance or evasion to be a *moral* one. As for the sexual aspect: the son of some friends of mine, living in a conservative eastern community, complained soon after he was drafted that girls who had formerly gone out with him would no longer do so. The old taunt of "Why aren't you in uniform?" has become the opposite: "Why aren't you in Sweden or in jail?" Soldiers on leave these days wear mufti.

Again, certain broad, vague expressions of patriotic

sentiment that in 1945 would have been considered commendable and in 1963 at least harmless have now become specifically distasteful to many as indicative of "extremist" beliefs. To a liberal—and liberals, on political record, are something like half of our voters—the display of a bumper sticker reading "Honor America" now suggests that the owner of the car is a full-fledged reactionary, ready to jail dissenters against the war and to use atomic weapons in its prosecution. "Support Your Local Police," which until a few years ago might have been an advertisement for a cake-sale benefit, now suggests racial prejudice. Even more to the point, display of the American flag itself in many unofficial settings has come to have disturbing implications. I confess, with some reluctance, that a flag decal posted in the window of a car or a barbershop now arouses in me feelings of hostility toward the owner. It would emphatically not have done so in 1945.

True enough, the practice called flag-waving has been in bad repute in sophisticated American circles for generations. But the expression was metaphorical, usually referring to overly florid oratory. That the display of the flag itself should come to suggest extremist political and social views is surely an anomaly without precedent. Try to imagine any other democratically ruled nation in which such a condition exists—or ever has existed.

The reason behind these changes is hardly obscure. On V-J Day we were triumphantly concluding a war in which the moral imperative had been clear to just about everyone. On the one hand our territory had been attacked in the Pacific, and on the other a barbaric aggressor who clearly represented a threat to us as well as to our allies was at large in Europe. Now we are engaged in a military adventure in a distant country in which I believe tortuous logic is required to find the threat to ourselves and in which, threats aside, the moral imperative is certainly not clear to many millions. Is the change, then, only temporary and expedient—like, say, the 1930's pacifism of my generation? I rather think not.

The computer revolution, filtering through from technology to culture, has recently come to change ways of thinking, perhaps more than we usually realize. Norman Macrae, deputy editor of the British *Economist*, commented after a recent U.S. visit on "the greater air of professionalism which runs through all ranks of American society; the greater instinct among ordinary individuals to say 'Now here is a problem, how can I solve it by a systematic approach?'" We have learned that computers can not only imitate the human brain (play chess, choose marriage partners) but can in many ways far exceed it (retrieve material from huge library collections or scan the contents of a fat telephone book in a fraction of a second; predict election results in an instant; put men on the moon). Is it not logical, then, that we should try to improve our minds by making them as much like computers as possible? The young executive or computer programmer who has learned the meaning and value of the systems approach to problems tries to apply it in every area of his personal life—in choosing schools for his children, in mowing his lawn, in pleasing his wife. It may well be that the current cult of irrationality is partly a reaction against this computer-spawned mimicry of mechanical thinking in everyday life.

Whether or not television and its concomitants in mass communications and world travel have done what Marshall McLuhan says they have—destroyed the "linear" habit of thinking imposed by the printed page and returned the whole world to the instinctual communication methods of the primitive tribal village—they have, it seems evident enough, changed our living and thinking habits in the direction of passive receptivity. I suggest that, with the first generation of television children now coming of age, we are just beginning to feel the force of this change.

While the Negro-rights movement has passed through its various stages—full integration of the armed forces (1948), the fight for integration of schools and public facilities (1954 *et seq.*), and finally "black power"—white attitudes toward aid to the Negro cause have gone through a spectrum of changes. In 1945 the majority of us, to judge from our actions, still clung to the thought that such aid through federal intervention was unnecessary or inappropriate. During the civil-rights decade beginning in 1954 most of us permitted ourselves to think of such aid as morally commendable on our part—that is to say, to think of it as having at least a component of charity. Now, in the black-power era when integration as a goal and the possible perfectability of American society are being increasingly rejected by the more militant black leaders, it has been borne in on more and more of us that giving things to minorities is and always was at best mere political expediency and at worst blackmail. Such ideas were unthinkable for nearly everyone in 1945; for all but a few in 1964. (President Johnson, it is interesting to note, was very much in the avant-garde of American thought in 1965 when he said at Howard University, "You do not wipe away the scars of centuries by saying, 'Now, you are free to go where you want, do what you desire, and choose the leaders you please.' You do not take a man who, for years, has been hobbled by chains, liberate him, bring him to the starting line of the race, saying, 'You are free to compete with the others. . . .'" Might not those words—had they not been spoken by an American President—serve as a black-power slogan?)

Along with the change in white attitudes toward blacks is a profound and unsettling change in the attitude of liberals toward our national history. Blacks and others, but mainly blacks, have persuaded liberals that ours is in crucial ways a racist society, and that it always has been. Formerly we thought of the American past, broadly, in terms of rural individualism, fanatical independence, and anti-intellectualism combined with visceral folk wisdom and an inherent sense of fairness—thought of it, that is, in a way that was both affectionate and patronizing. We minimized or dismissed particular instances of racism (lynchings, the Scottsboro case, or the wartime detention camps for Nisei) as being confined to a particular geographical area or attributable to the bad judgment of particular leaders. Now, for many Americans, almost any tintype glimpse of the American past—the village band concert with its handful of tentatively smiling black faces in the back row, the political rally with no black faces anywhere—suggests racism. To a degree our history has been poisoned for us. And I believe that the consequences of this, in the light of our current national demoralization, can hardly be overemphasized at this time in America's life.

Our leaders themselves have become demoralized to an extent surely without precedent since the Civil War. "We know our lakes are dying, our rivers growing filthier daily, our atmosphere increasingly polluted," John Gardner, former Cabinet member and more recently head of the Urban Coalition, said not long ago. "We are aware of racial tensions that could tear the nation apart. We understand that oppressive poverty in the midst of affluence is intolerable. We see that our cities are sliding toward disaster. . . . But we are seized by a kind of paralysis of the will." Does not such language, in the nation of Fourth of July oratory, and coming from not just an Establishment figure but to some *the* Establishment figure of the present moment, represent a clear break with the past, even the very recent past?

Naturally, the demoralization of the leaders is felt among the people. "Most people no longer seem to care—if, indeed, they know—what is happening to their country," Richard Harris wrote late last year in *The New Yorker* magazine. "Exhausted by the demands of modern life and muddled by the fearful discord tearing at society, they seem to have turned their common fate over to their leaders in a way that would have been inconceivable five years ago." But when the leaders talk of paralysis of the will, who will lead?

I come now to recent changes in attitudes and values among the young, where we may find a key to what is happening to the country. To review briefly, then, the most obvious manifestations of these changes:

Youth on the campus has discovered its previously unsuspected and therefore untested power to change its environment and the conditions of its life. From the Berkeley revolt (1964) to the one at Columbia (1968) to the one at Harvard (1969) we have seen the content of such campus uprisings gradually broaden from demands for the right to use dirty words to demands for changes in the course of study, insistence on sexual and other forms of personal freedom, demands for revision of admissions policies, and ultimatums about the reorganization of entire curricula. The rebels have developed their own jargon—largely mindless and question-begging like all political jargon: in pursuit of "restructuring" (getting their own way) the dissidents resort to "confrontation" (violence or the threat of it), make "nonnegotiable demands" (refuse to engage in reasonable discussion), and, if they get what they want, sometimes complain with what seems to be a certain disappointment that they have been "co-opted" (yielded to). A comical aspect of their behavior is that they frequently ask those

in authority to help them revolt against that very authority; they want, for example, to be offered formal courses in the techniques of campus disruption as well as guerrilla warfare. (A university president told me recently of a student delegation that had come to ask him, not without an attractive diffidence, that he help them by giving them the benefit of his political experience. "What they wanted me to help them rebel against was *me*," he commented.) But campus revolts are not a joke. They are evidence of an idea completely new in the United States, poles apart from the passive orthodoxy of the silent generation of a decade earlier, that teaching authority is not absolute but fluid and malleable, that the young can move the sun and the moon in their heavens if they try, that their universe in spite of its ordered surface is basically anarchic. And the authorities, by yielding to them again and again, have confirmed their most disturbing suspicions.

Recent statistics compiled by the Urban Research Corporation of Chicago give a striking picture of how widespread campus revolts have been. Covering 232 campuses over the first half of 1969, the study showed that during that period 215,000 students, or about one tenth of all those enrolled at the institutions studied, actively participated in a total of nearly three hundred major protests—all in just six months. Before the fact that only one student in ten was active in the uprisings is taken to indicate that the youth revolt is just the phenomenon of a small but visible minority, we would do well to consider that historically the passive sympathizers with new movements have usually far outnumbered the activists.

The young have turned against careers in business, particularly in big and long-established business, to such an extent that some campus recruiters have expressed concern as to where the managers of the future will come from—although up to now there have been enough exceptions to keep the business schools from being depopulated and the lower ranks of corporate management from being undermanned.

They have made a cult of irrationality, what with astrology, Oriental occultism, and above all the use of drugs. ("*We* never needed drugs to drive us crazy," the middle-aged social commentator David T. Bazelon once told me.) This tendency runs deep and wide, cutting across economic, social, and intellectual lines among the young. The sheltered, conservatively brought-up white southern darling and the would-be hippie son of liberal northern suburbanites yearn alike for the experience of New York City's East Village, and the young Harvard intellectual is almost as likely as the high-school dropout to express or imply hostility to the traditional intellectual materials, abstract ideas, and rational comment. Curiously, the defense of irrationality is often put—persuasively—on rational grounds: that logical thought in foreign policy led to Vietnam, that logical thought in economic development led to pollution, and so on.

The young are apparently in the process of radically redefining sex roles. The question of which forces (the Pill, the obscenity explosion in the media set off by the courts' anticensorship decisions, or the general air of permissiveness in the land) have brought about a radical change in sexual customs among both the young and their elders, remains undecided. No one really knows. What is much clearer, and perhaps more interesting, is that the traditional aggressiveness of the young American male about his maleness, which has so often led to anti-intellectualism, Babbittry, and cultural self-deprivation in general—for example, the American he-man's hostility to most of the arts on grounds that they are effete—seems to have been emphatically reversed. The short hair and pointedly different clothing that he always used to set himself unmistakably apart from girls are more and more being abandoned in favor of long hair, fur coats, beads, and other adornments that were formerly considered feminine. The American male's dread of appearing to be unmanly seems to be lessening. More significantly, one is struck by the new sense of community that boys and girls feel. The growing insistence of the young on coeducation is not just a matter of having sex available but one of principle, growing out of a new conviction that the sexes are not so different as American culture has decreed them to be and that the old segregation is therefore absurd.

The symptoms I have been recording are, of course, parts of a syndrome, and one that may be viewed in two diametrically opposed ways. Looked at in a favorable light, the new youth are gentle, loving, natural, intuitive, opposed only to war and obsession with money, to hypocrisy and the other agreed-upon weaknesses of modern society as organized by their elders. In a different perspective they represent progressive-school permissiveness and self-indulgence run wild: their causes are merely self-serving (opposition to the draft, for example), their attitudes are self-righteous ("Just because you are growing older do not be afraid of change," they gravely lecture their parents and teachers), their manners are deplorable or nonexistent, their minds are flabby, their herding together indicates fear of standing alone, and the manner of their protests sometimes appears ominously antidemocratic. Macrae of *The Economist* goes so far as to say that some of the actions of black-power and radical white students during the winter of 1968–69 "invited the most direct comparison with the way that Hit-

ler's brownshirts operated in the Weimar Republic." On the other hand Ralph Nader's consumer-protection crusade, which clearly appeals strongly to the brightest and most idealistic among the young, might fairly be described as passionately *pro*democratic in that its aim is to save that most characteristic democratic institution, the business corporation, from its own shortcomings. Paradoxes and contradictions, then; and it is quite possible—indeed, perhaps it is inevitable—for a liberal of the previous generation to see the young in both lights at the same time.

For such an observer, analysis is more profitable than judgment. Consider, then, the vital statistics. The median age of the American population at present is a bit under twenty-eight years. Half of us, roughly speaking, were born before the middle of World War II and half since it. Half of us were of an age to be percipient before V-J Day, and half were not. The distinction is not arbitrary, because it was with the end of the war that the new era, the modern world, began. The time has come when "over thirty" means precisely "born before the war." Only the younger half of the American people have never known the world of traditional values as it was without the disrupters of those values—television, computers, jet travel, space travel, the threat of nuclear extinction. Only the younger half truly belong to the new world—that is, accept it instinctively, without mental or emotional effort, because they have not any old world to compare it with.

And consider this: the five postwar moods before the present one were conjoined as well as consecutive—each had its roots in reaction to the previous one, as have the moods of most nations through most of past history. Wartime family disruptions led logically and naturally to early postwar domesticity. The Cold War, which really began in 1945 at Yalta, bore its bitter fruit five years later in Korea. Armed conflict with our former allies, the Communists, led logically to the era of suspicion. The eventual relaxation of that crisis cleared the way for the Eisenhower years of self-indulgence. And the new energy and responsibility of the Kennedy term was clearly enough a reaction to that. In such a linear way did our history unfold for almost two decades.

And then—snap! The chain of events seemed to be broken. Suddenly we flew off in directions that seemed to be neither a continuation of nor a reaction to anything that had gone before. Disillusion with uniform and flag did not appear to be rooted in reaction to any particular superpatriotism of the preceding period; mechanized thinking was not new, but the existence, indeed the ubiquitous presence, of actual thinking machines was; the new youth rebellion could be seen as a reaction to youth passivity a decade earlier, but the breadth and depth of the response was so far out of proportion to the challenge as to make such an explanation seem entirely inadequate. The present American mood, then, in many of its aspects, has had no precedents or antecedents; it represents almost a clear break; it seems to have come out of the blue. Meanwhile, let us remember, it has not been accompanied by sharp breaks in or reversals of the broad ameliorative trends that have marched through the whole postwar period. There are no jolts or breaks around 1964 or 1965 in the charts of social progress. The nation seems to have changed its mind, or to be in the process of changing its mind, on many of the most basic matters for no immediately discernible material reason. And this occurs precisely at the time when the new post-V-J Day generation is coming of age.

Can this conjunction of facts be more than coincidental? Indeed, must it not be? If so, then the new generation, the generation that is in tune with the new world because it never knew the old one, appears, for better or worse, as the basic force behind the new, unprecedented American attitudes. As for the statistical charts, their relatively smooth continuance through this period of violent cultural upheaval may be explained by the fact that the charts and the things recorded in the charts—matters of business, government, philanthropy—remain in the hands of the old postwar generation. It does not really live in the new world it has made, yet it still nervously holds all the levers of national power.

One who accepts such an analysis is Margaret Mead. In her recent book, *Culture and Commitment: A Study of the Generation Gap*, she declares that "our present situation is unique, without any parallel in the past," and that—not just in the United States but world-wide—the human race is arriving through the youth revolt at an entirely new phase of cultural evolution. Putting her argument in a context of rigorous anthropological study rather than in the familiar one of parlor sociology, she describes the new phase as a "prefigurative" society: one in which the traditional handing down of knowledge and belief from the elder generation to the younger is being reversed and in which "it will be the child and not the parent or grandparent that represents what is to come." No longer anywhere in the world, Dr. Mead says, can the elders, born before the Second World War, know and understand what the children know and understand: "Even very recently the elders could say, 'You know, I have been young and you never have been old.' But today's young people can reply, 'You never have been young in the world I am young in, and you never can be.'" The prefigurative society she sees emerging is, Dr. Mead says, the first one in human history.

It is a persuasive case, and, fitted together with the vital statistics I have cited, it leads to a persuasive explanation of why changes in our values and attitudes, after years of poking along like a donkey cart in a time of great transformation in our material situation, have recently taken off as steeply as a jet plane. So it comes about that the elders—whether they conservatively wring their hands over the new changes or liberally try to understand, absorb, and temper them—feel like expatriate visitors in their own country. Like expatriates, we of the prewar generation are inclined to spend our days wavering between wonder, exasperation, apprehension, disgust, and superiority toward what we see around us. Again like expatriates, we tend to cling together in enclaves, to propitiate our sense of loneliness by finding islands of our own within the new world that conform as closely as possible to the old one. The turned-on headlights of daytime drivers that have been so familiar a sight in many parts of the country in recent months are supposed to mean support of our Vietnam policy, but they mean more than that. They are a symbol by which the loneliest of the lonely expatriates reassure themselves that they are not wholly alone; they are the club ties of the American Club in Samarkand.

Even if the analysis is right, all of this is, of course, a change still in process, and indeed still in an early stage of process, rather than an accomplished fact. The "silent majority" apparently still *is* a majority—of poll respondents and of voters—and even if it were not, traditional methods of succession to power have survived up to now to the extent that the older generation would still hold business and government power and might be expected to continue to do so for some years to come. Even among the young themselves Dr. Mead's prefigurative culture is still very far from universal. There are whole campuses in "middle America" where a long-haired boy is an object of derision, where revolt against university authority never crosses anyone's mind, where books and magazines containing four-letter words are missing from the library shelves, and where "God Bless America" is sung without irony.

But such attitudes among the postwar generation seem to represent cultural lag. They are scarcely the wave of the future. It is those older than the nation's median age who make up the bulk of the silent majority. In purely actuarial terms, this majority is living on borrowed time; it is a majority under a death sentence.

What happens next?

One line of thought holds that the strange new attitudes and values are attributable not to the influence of youth but to the Vietnam war and the disruptions, frustrations, and loss of morale attendant upon it—its ability, as James Reston of the *New York Times* has written, to "poison everything." This interpretation is reassuring to the prewar generation because it implies that when the war is over everything will revert to the way it was before. But those born in the years immediately after V-J Day, who were entering college when the Vietnam war was escalated and are leaving it now, and who have lived only in the strange new world, can scarcely be expected to go back where they have never been. I am convinced that Vietnam is not the root cause of our current malaise and that if there had been no Vietnam the young would have found plenty of other reasons to dissociate themselves violently from their elders and their elders' regime. Certainly the end of the war, when it blessedly comes, will mark the end of our current paralysis and the beginning of a seventh and more hopeful postwar mood; but I expect it to be a mood not of returning to the familiar but of pushing forward to something new and unknown. In the traditional American cultural pattern youth has always been allowed its fling with the tacit understanding between youngsters and elders that after graduation the youngsters would "put away childish things" and "settle down." The wild young buck who had been proud of his capacity for beer and beer-inspired pranks would sink quickly into sober, hard-working domesticity, and the pretty blonde who had found it amusing to flirt with Communism while in college would become his meekly Republican, upwardly mobile bride. It is impossible for me to imagine the post-V-J Day generation following this familiar pattern. One can, for example, visualize their male hairstyle going from shoulder length to shaved heads—but not to crew cuts; one can visualize their politics doing a flip-flop to dangerously radical rightist positions—but not to traditional conservatism or traditional liberalism.

How, then, can they be expected to react to being older and to assuming power and responsibility instead of defying them? Will they, in their turn, be "prefigured" by the new younger generation that will consist of their children? How will they run the Ford Foundation? the Institute for Advanced Study? the Bureau of the Census? Will they continue the broad liberal trends initiated by the older generation that they now revile—trends toward more social-minded corporations, better-distributed wealth, more general education, less pervasive bigotry? Will they bring to reality *The Economist*'s prophecy that "the United States in this last third of the twentieth century is the place where man's long economic problem is ending"? Will, say, the affairs of General Motors be managed by men (or women) wearing long hair and beads and smoking pot during sales conferences? Or will there be no General Motors?

The fact that it sounds like material for a musical-comedy skit indicates how little we know what to expect. Adolf A. Berle said recently, speaking of economic and social affairs in the United States, "We are beginning to evolve a new ball game." Whether we like it or not, the rules of the new game will not be our rules. They will be devised by those born since V-J Day.

John Brooks's disturbing article serves as a grim postscript to his book The Great Leap: The Past Twenty-Five Years in America, *published in 1966. Mr. Brooks is a staff writer for* The New Yorker, *and his most recent book is* Once in Golconda: A True Drama of Wall Street, 1920–1938.

How to Run an Empire

CONTINUED FROM PAGE 45

Islands. Make quite certain that when the peace protocols are written you are given in South Vietnam whatever facilities you require for exerting influence in that area. If it's the peace of the world you wish to secure, the *Pax Americana* cannot be guaranteed from within Fortress America. Every empire, from the Roman to our own, repeats that lesson. World power cannot be exercised by any nation unless she goes beyond her own frontiers. Only one empire can resist another. Within decades of your retreat behind your own stockade, much of the world, and certainly all the East, will have fallen under Communist control.

What indeed is so morally wrong about American flags among palm and pine? Pure self-determination could only logically apply if nations consisted of one race, long established within natural ethnic frontiers. The nations which answer to that description are few and far between. Every single boundary in Africa was artificially drawn during the nineteenth century in some European foreign ministry. What *moral* right have the Spaniards and Portuguese in South America? Or Romanian Jews in Israel? Why do the Soviets rule in Samarkand? Why is the government of an independent Mauritius given to the immigrant Indian community? In each case, the answer is simple—no moral right at all. The Spaniards and Portuguese conquered the territories and killed the natives; the Jews settled and now defend their settlements; the Russians extended their empire overland to the east; the Indians are the most numerous and vote for each other. There are no morals about it. Americans, as part of their imperial duty, must spread and multiply. If they care to play to the gallery by granting statehood to Puerto Rico or erecting an elaborate Potemkin façade of independence in front of Panama, that's their business. It's always sensible to undermine your opponent's arguments by conforming to what is called "world opinion," however ill-founded. Even the Russians have allowed the Baltic states to keep their languages and folk songs and national costumes. What does it matter who dances on the village green, as long as every function of government is in Russian hands?

And if you leave your military bases around the world, or reduce them to the extent that your power is no longer credible, do you believe any Western nation or concert of nations will take your place? Do you believe the Russians will disarm in harmony? Are you prepared to allow the Communist world to spread right up to the walls of Fortress America, confident that the American dream can remain inviolate inside? You know perfectly well that it is only American arms, money, and men, Ameri-can purpose and command, that keeps the military alliances of the Western world alive. Your allies are in any case the most reluctant of military partners, continually basing their military plans on the protection of what they call the "American umbrella." Without you they will dither and fall apart and spend their budgets on pills and permissiveness, exactly as the slack kingdoms of Europe would have remained supine under Napoleon had not England provided an injection of gold and steel.

Your influence on the Western and Christian world is, however, your most precious and most powerful weapon. But your golden calf has become suspect: you literally need a new image. Norman Rockwell's well-fed families of the "White Christmas" era were too complacent, too narrow, much too pleased with themselves. Even moderate intellectuals were contemptuous of Babbitt's passionate salesmanship. Overseas admirers of the American Presidency after four White House occupants of the Roosevelt, Truman, Eisenhower, Kennedy calibre were shaken out of their admiration by reports of the personal crudity and public credibility gap of Lyndon Johnson. Outside America, the Nixon era's space flights appeal only to a narrow and rather sophisticated minority. Stupendous as your achievements have been, most humble people would prefer to see America making a greater concentration of effort on human problems. As for your youth, inevitable as is their reaction to the grey flannel suit, they are reacting in a way which is very alarming for anyone who believes in evolution. What is wrong with the old American puritanism tempered with the best of the new educated liberal beliefs? You will be opposing, as long as this century lasts or longer, the most formidably puritan dogma, the Marxist-Leninist creed. As the English found during the last war that they were obliged to become more organised, more methodical, more Germanic than the Germans in order to defeat their enemy, so you too must become more austere than 1970 finds you if you are to convince your own youth and their fellows in the Western world that you can offer an American society worth working for, sacrificing for, and if need be, dying for.

The most important attitude you must change is your attitude to time. You have an adolescent's attitude to time. It is not hurrying to the extent you think it is. A European reads with amazement constant references to recent years as if they were part of a vanished age. "Way back in 1953 . . ." begins a typical American magazine article, usually trumpeting the tremendous strides made since that misty era. "Way back in 1453" is admissible, but sixteen years is a drop in the ocean of time. It all stems from the passionate desire of each American that the millennium should occur during his lifetime. He is creating a materialistic heaven-on-earth and must be alive to enjoy it. Anything that detracts from the creation of this heaven, or diverts the creator's attention, is an extraneous nuisance, a "problem" to be "solved" as soon as possible so that he can return to the real business of life. So the Vietnam war, the crime wave, racial tension, youthful protest, must be solved, settled, and shelved before the next election, the next summit meeting, the beginning of the 1970's, the renewal of an international loan. Such an attitude hands you tied and bound to anyone who can afford to wait. It is a crippling handicap in your negotiations with the Communists. Remember the old German proverb about Russia: "In that country a hundred miles is no distance, a hundred deaths no tragedy, a hundred years no time." You are dealing, you Americans, with that kind of people, and at times they are playing with you. Life, as Harold Macmillan reminded Ed Murrow in their famous television interview, does not consist of problems that can be solved but of situations with which you must live. Don't be so impatient. Time is only your enemy if you misconstrue its meaning. On many a reputation, shattered in Vietnam, could be written the ancient epitaph: "Here lies the man who tried to hurry the East."

Consider some domestic American institutions. It is still undeniable that in a world which governs its international behaviour with more attention to old-fashioned morality than many newspapers would have us believe, an empire must give an example to its satellites if she wishes those satellites to fall into line. She must insist on certain standards—not to the extent that Russia has imposed her standards on Czechoslovakia, but perhaps as closely as we, the British, insisted on standards in public life in India and Africa. I would advise what in your jargon is called a long hard look at some of the less attractive aspects of the American scene—the administration of justice, not always impartial; the respect for law and order, not always enforced; the standards of political life, not always incorrupt; the equality of the citizen, not always upheld; the rights of the individual, not always respected; the denial of privilege, not always observed. In America there are too many ideals cloaking too much cynicism; too many robber barons oppressing too many poor; too much mere talk about peace and too many acts of violence. Perhaps a military defeat will be a good moral purge. It may allow you to rekindle a feeling for America which foreigners have lost. We fear you, we envy you, sometimes we like you, but we have lost a lot of our respect for you. The "American Way of Life" has become a bit of a giggle. We would like you more if you stood higher in our esteem.

Yet although the main foundations of empire are laid at home, may I offer two specific pieces of advice which concern those Americans who are most often found in the imperial outposts. Encourage—and I make no bones about using this Nancy Mitford language—a better class of person to become officers in your armed forces. In an empire the military needs prestige. As your representatives abroad, senior officers require something more than bonhomie and set opinions. Your present incumbents—devoted and technically adept though they may be—include a number of the illiberal and ill-educated. The military men's power and influence is too wide for them to be any but the best you breed.

Improve too the quality of the men who represent your nation's mass media as foreign correspondents. The ease with which Vietnam press visas were granted to American and foreigner alike may well turn out to be one of the major mistakes of the conflict. Some of my own most vivid memories of being a Saigon-based war correspondent concerned American reporters who either so loathed their country's war policy or were so blindly in love with the exhilaration of battle that their objectivity was seriously impaired. I also recall many examples of gross and insensitive behaviour by pressmen—such as a photographer who arrived on a scene of appalling carnage and asked in an enthusiastic tone, "Any K.I.A. [killed in action] from Dayton?" Without in any way suggesting that censorship should have been imposed, or without wishing to impugn the many outstanding reporters who went to Vietnam, I nevertheless believe that America did herself a disservice by not being more careful about who was licensed to cover that war.

There—that is enough; indeed, it may be too much, so lest you think my damns have been too constant and my praise too faint, let me end on a note of sincere admiration. I know of no people who are so open and ready to criticism, or who examine themselves so honestly, as do civilised Americans. Imagine a Czech journalist writing for *Novosti* in the language I have used. There is, too, a type of American civilisation which is the more attractive because it is still evolving. It is a civilisation at once enquiring, active, liberal, lettered, and unhurried, forming a kernel of real culture and taste. I know men who belong to what is plainly becoming an American aristocracy—though they would shy away from the word—in its best sense: leaders, rulers, thinkers, reformers, men of will and purpose and courage. If these men become the new American imperialists, the world will be better and more quietly governed, for they know how to carry the big stick, while walking softly as well.

Many readers, especially younger ones, will doubtless disagree with the author, but they cannot fault Mr. Aitken on his age. He is twenty-seven, a staff member of the London Evening Standard, *and currently a Conservative candidate for Parliament. He is a great-nephew of the publisher Lord Beaverbrook and grandson of an old Empire hand, Lord Rugby, who once governed Peshawar and the Sudan and was permanent secretary of the Colonial Office.*

From their wheel chairs F.D.R.'s fellow patients at Warm Springs bade a last farewell to their friend as a hearse carried his body away.

F.D.R.

CONTINUED FROM PAGE 11

to our realization of tomorrow will be our doubts of today. Let us move forward with strong and active faith.

Warm Springs on Thursday morning, April 12, 1945, was sunny and pleasant. Dogwood and wild violets bloomed along the road to Pine Mountain. There, at his favorite picnic spot, friends of Franklin Roosevelt were preparing a barbecue for the late afternoon; the smells of honeysuckle and stewing beef and chicken mingled in the soft Georgia air. A wooden armchair was set out for the guest of honor under a wisteria-laden oak tree, placed so that he could gaze at the greening valley below.

Down in the valley, in his corner bedroom in the Little White House, the President was sitting in bed reading the Atlanta *Constitution;* the big-city newspapers from the North had been delayed by bad weather in Washington. The headlines reported American troops fifty-seven miles from Berlin and 115 miles from the Russians; a big fleet of super-Forts had bombed Tokyo in daylight. Roosevelt looked up from his paper at the sound of chatter in the kitchen. He called out to Lizzie McDuffie, who was dusting the living room. What were they talking about? Lizzie came to the door. Mr. Roosevelt had always had time to talk with her, to answer her questions.

"Well, Mr. Roosevelt, do you believe in reincarnation?" Did *she* believe in it? he countered. She didn't know, Lizzie said, but if there was such a thing she wanted to come back as a canary bird.

"A *canary bird!*" The President looked at her two-hundred-pound frame, threw his paper down, and burst out laughing. Lizzie McDuffie would never forget that: the President with his head thrown back, his eyes closed, laughing and exclaiming—as she had heard him do a hundred times—"Don't you love it? Don't you *love* it?"

When Hassett reached the Little White House around noon with the delayed mail pouch, Roosevelt was sitting in the living room in his leather armchair chatting with his cousins Margaret Suckley and Laura Delano and with Mrs. Winthrop Rutherfurd.* Two years before, Lucy Mercer Rutherfurd had commissioned a portrait painter, Elizabeth Shoumatoff, to do a water color of the President; recently he had asked the artist to paint another picture of him as a gift to Lucy's daughter. Madame Shoumatoff came in while Roosevelt was signing a sheaf of appointments and awards Hassett had put before him—signing them as usual with a wide, flowing pen, so that Hassett had to spread them out to dry. The usual banter followed about putting out Hassett's "laundry." One document was a bill just passed by Congress to continue the Commodity Credit Corporation and increase its borrowing power. The President signed it with a flourish, telling the ladies, "Here's where I make a law."

Hassett looked on disapprovingly as the painter set up her easel, measured Roosevelt's nose, asked him to turn back and forth. His boss looked much too weary for all this, he felt. He collected the signed documents and departed, leaving the President with some papers to read while he was being sketched. The room was quiet now. The artist continued her work, but the President became so intent in his reading that he fell out of his pose. She used the time to fill in colors. At one o'clock the President looked at his watch.

"We've got just fifteen minutes more." The house-boy was setting the dining table on the other side of the room. Margaret Suckley continued to crochet, Laura Delano to fill vases with flowers. Lucy Rutherfurd watched the President. He made a little joke and looked into her

---

*An assistant to Mrs. Roosevelt and intimate friend of Franklin Roosevelt during the World War I years, Lucy Mercer had later married Winthrop Rutherfurd. She and Roosevelt re-established their old friendship during World War II.

The hearse pulled into the Warm Springs station where the President's coffin was placed in the rear car of the waiting funeral train.

smiling face. He lit a cigarette and studied his papers.

The fifteen minutes were almost up when the President raised his left hand to his temple, dropped it limply, then raised and pressed it behind his neck. He said very quietly: "I have a terrific headache." Then his arm dropped, his head fell to the left, his body slumped. A call went out to Dr. Bruenn, who had been sunning himself at the pool. When Bruenn arrived, the President was still slumped in his chair; only with difficulty was the heavy, inert body carried into the bedroom. The President's breathing stopped, then started again in great snoring gasps. Bruenn sheared away his clothes, injected papaverine and amyl nitrate, and telephoned Rear Admiral Ross T. McIntire, the President's personal physician, in Washington. Madame Shoumatoff had already left with Mrs. Rutherfurd. Hassett arrived and knew the end was near when he heard the awful labored breathing. Grace Tully sat quietly in a corner of the living room, her lips moving in prayer. The minutes ticked by; the breathing grew more tortured; then it stopped. Bruenn could hear no heart sounds. He injected adrenalin into the heart muscle. No response. At 3:55 P.M. Dr. Bruenn pronounced him dead.

Grace Tully walked into the bedroom, kissed the President lightly on the forehead, then walked out onto the porch and stood there wordless and tearless. The reporters were summoned from the barbecue on Pine Mountain. They swept into the little house. Hassett was standing near the center of the living room. "Gentlemen," he said quietly, "it is my sad duty to inform you that the President of the United States is dead. . . ."

The news came to Churchill in his study at 10 Downing Street just before midnight; for a long time he sat stunned and silent, feeling as though he had been struck a physical blow. In Moscow, Ambassador Averell Harriman was awakened at 2 A.M.; he drove to the Kremlin to see Stalin, who seemed moved and preoccupied by the news as he held the envoy's hand for a long moment,

saying nothing. In Chungking, Generalissimo Chiang Kai-shek received the news as he began eating breakfast; he left the meal untouched and retired for mourning. In Japan an announcer for Radio Tokyo read the death bulletin and surprisingly presented some special music "in honor of the passing of a great man."

In Berlin the news came to Goebbels on the steps of the Propaganda Ministry just after a bombing attack. His exultant face could be seen in the light of the flames from the burning Chancellery across the Wilhelmplatz. He had been telling the Führer and others that Germany would be saved at the eleventh hour by an unexpected event, just as Frederick the Great had been saved by the death of the czarina two centuries before. He called for champagne and telephoned Hitler, who was in his deep bunker.

"My Führer! I congratulate you. Roosevelt is dead. It is written in the stars that the second half of April will be the turning point for us. This is Friday, April 13. It is the turning point!"

Next morning the army band and a thousand infantrymen from Fort Benning, black streamers flying from their colors, led the hearse between lines of helmeted paratroopers down the curving red clay road through the Warm Springs Foundation. Behind came Eleanor Roosevelt in an open car, the President's Scottie, Fala, at her feet. At Georgia Hall patients in wheel chairs waved farewell to the friend who had presided at their Thanksgiving dinners and swum with them in the warm pool. Graham Jackson had waited at the barbecue to play his accordion for the President; now, his face a map of anguish and disbelief, he stepped out from the columned portico and rendered "Going Home."

Its drums beating a steady, deadened roll, the procession wound down to the little railroad station. The heavy, flag-draped coffin was handed through a window into the rear car of the presidential train. There it rested on a pine box so low that only the top of the casket could

79

be seen through the windows. Four servicemen stood guard. The train started imperceptibly and began rolling down the track to Atlanta.

Eleanor Roosevelt sat in the presidential lounge car. The afternoon before, she had been at the White House when word came from Warm Springs that her husband had fainted; Admiral McIntire, in Washington, advised her to go ahead with a speaking engagement so that people would not be alarmed. She had done so, with her unquenchable sense of duty, only to be called back to the White House and told the definite news. She had had time to ask Harry Truman, "Is there anything we can do for *you*?"; to send a message to her four soldier sons, "He did his job to the end as he would want you to do." Then she had flown south with McIntire and Stephen Early, the President's press secretary.

While the train rolled through the gently billowing land of west central Georgia—his adopted state, Roosevelt called it—the world was trying to adjust to the death of the President. Almost everywhere the first reactions had been shock, incredulity, grief, and fear. Now it was time for second thoughts. Editorialists struggled to capture the nature of the man, the meaning of his life, the measure of the loss.

It was no easy task, for even those who knew Roosevelt best agreed that he was a man infinitely complex and almost incomprehensible. On such a relatively simple matter as his behavior toward fellow human beings he oscillated; like all men, he was both generous and vindictive, but it was Roosevelt's mixture of the two qualities that was so baffling. Even now, friends of Al Smith were remembering how Roosevelt had befriended him during the war years and tried to bail out his Empire State Building, even though the "Happy Warrior" had scathingly attacked the New Deal. And Henry Luce, who had not treated the President ungently, was suddenly and arbitrarily barred by the White House from touring the Pacific Theater; he would hate Roosevelt to his dying day. The President could get along with anyone he wanted to, from Stalin to MacArthur to Huey Long to the man in the street. People in Warm Springs remembered the time he was driving his little car through the town and had stopped and waved over a Negro walking by; how the "colored man was scared, scraping his feet and all. . . . Then, first you know, he was leaning on the President's automobile, throwing his arms around like he was talking to anybody." Yet people as different as Jim Farley and Dean Acheson felt that he condescended—that he conveyed, Acheson felt, much of the attitude of European royalty.

South of Gainesville, Georgia, black women in a cotton field saw the train coming and fell to their knees in supplication. It was remarkable, this human touch of the President's, but sometimes his charm had an edge of coquetry and pretense. Marshal Sir William Sholto-Douglas, of the R.A.F., remembered how Roosevelt had greeted him with a lecture on Scottish history and the achievements of the Douglases, told how he had a Scottish grandmother himself, and so on. Douglas sensed an indefinable flaw in his manner; he felt that he was witnessing some kind of performance—still, he was moved to the point of tears, and Roosevelt, he confessed later, nearly had him eating out of his hand. Jesse Jones, just fired from the administration, told a reporter that the President was a hypocrite and lacking in character but "you just can't help liking that fellow."

Along with all his democratic manner and instincts he had that curious interest in royal and noble personages and doings. He told a friend, rather improbably, that he had been hurt in England after the first war when he had not been invited to Buckingham Palace. In a different vein, and most curiously, he allowed and even encouraged Adolf Berle to call him "Caesar" in addressing the President in private. Berle, who was always bemused by the irony of power, was still calling him this the last time he saw Roosevelt, just after Yalta. Did the President derive from the term some curious satisfaction that outweighed the risk of his enemies' discovering it and gleefully publicizing it—or did he tolerate Berle's fun because he enjoyed imagining what they would do if they *did* find out about it?

Night came, and the funeral train—blacked out except for the ghostly, half-lit rear coach—wove slowly back and forth through the Carolina piedmont. Looking out from her berth at the countryside her husband loved, Eleanor Roosevelt glimpsed the solemn faces of the crowds at the depots and crossroads. The train would arrive in Washington eighty years to the day after Lincoln was shot. Eleanor remembered Millard Lampell's poem "The Lonesome Train":

> *A lonesome train on a lonesome track,*
> *Seven coaches painted black. . . .*
> *A slow train, a quiet train,*
> *Carrying Lincoln home again. . . .*

Perhaps it was in Roosevelt's home that the main clues to his character lay. William James, borrowing from Cardinal Newman, at one time spoke of the "once-born," those who easily fitted into the ideology of their time, and of those "sick souls" and "divided selves" who went through a second birth, seizing on a second ideology. Roosevelt was one of the once-born. His identity was formed in a harmonious and stable family; he moved securely and surely from the pedestal of the only child of doting parents into the wider but equally untroubled environments of Hyde Park, Groton, and Harvard friendships. If his loving references to his Hyde Park home were not revealing enough of his sense of identity and of roots, his habit all through his Presidency of reducing policies and programs to terms of home and family would have betrayed his thinking: thus the Good Neighbor policy, the Big Four constables or policemen, the Lend-Lease "garden hose"; his idea that new institutions like the United Nations must toddle like a child for a few years before gaining strength; his repeated references to heads of state sitting around the table like members of the same family, or like neighbors; and his suggestion on at least one occasion that the best way to keep peace in a family—he was referring to de Gaulle and the other Frenchmen—was to keep the members of the family *apart*.

With an assurance undergirded by his sense of identity, Roosevelt moved from Groton and Harvard into the muckraking decade of Theodore Roosevelt, into the simmering politics of the Hudson Valley, into the reformist and idealistic mood of the Wilson years. It was with this assurance, sometimes bordering on arrogance, that he could confront and overcome his domestic adversaries of the 1930's—and do so without personal hatred for a Huey Long, a Carter Glass, a Norman Thomas, an Al Smith, or a Wendell Willkie. He reserved his hatred for people in his own social world, such as Hamilton Fish, who he felt had betrayed him; and they reciprocated.

He embraced the ideology of freedom not with the demonic passion of the true believer who possesses a creed and ends up being possessed by it, but with the easy assurance of a man who slowly fashions his political faith, borrowing from the thinkers and political leaders of the day, reshaping his ideas as he undergoes new experiences and lives through changing times—and hence can, when necessary, keep his distance from that faith's possessive demands. He overcame his adversaries not only because he outwitted and outmaneuvered and outstayed them but also because he outsermonized and outmoralized them. Only a man deadly serious and supremely self-assured could have spent the time Roosevelt did appealing to old-fashioned moralisms of home and school, the golden rule and the Ten Commandments as interpreted by Endicott Peabody (the headmaster of Groton), the maxims of freedom as practiced by Wilson and Al Smith, the "simple rules of human conduct to which we always go back," as he said in 1932. So certain was he of the rightness of his aims that he was willing to use Machiavellian means to reach them; and his moral certainty made him all the more effective in the struggle. He used the tricks of the fox to serve the purposes of the lion.

People in northern Virginia and Washington felt they had never known such a lovely spring. On the warm and windless morning of Saturday, April 14, the lilacs and azaleas were in full bloom. The funeral train rolled through woods spattered with showers of dogwood,

crossed the Potomac, and pulled into Union Station. Thousands waited outside in the plaza, as they had so often before. Anna, Elliott, and Elliott's wife entered the rear car; President Truman and his Cabinet followed. Then the soldier's funeral procession began—armored troops, truck-borne infantry, the Marine band, a battalion of Annapolis midshipmen, the Navy band, WACS, WAVES, SPARS, women Marines, then a small, black-draped caisson carrying the coffin, drawn by six white horses, with a seventh serving as outrider. Army bombers thundered overhead.

"It was a processional of terrible simplicity and a march too solemn for tears," William S. White wrote, "except here and there where someone wept alone. It was a march, for all its restrained and slight military display, characterized not by this or by the thousands of flags that hung limply everywhere but by a mass attitude of unuttered, unmistakable prayer."

In front of the White House the coffin was lifted from the caisson during the playing of the national anthem, carried up the front steps, and wheeled down a long red carpet to the East Room. Here, where Lincoln had lain, banks of lilies covered the walls. The President, Cabinet members, Supreme Court justices, labor leaders, diplomats, politicians, agency heads, crowded into the room and spilled over into the Blue Room. At the close of his prayer Bishop Dun paused and quoted from F. D. R.'s First Inaugural: ". . . Let me assert my firm belief that the only thing we have to fear is fear itself. . . ."

Eleanor Roosevelt rose and left the room; then the others filed out. Later, upstairs, she came into Anna's room, in anguish. She had heard in Warm Springs, from a relative, about Lucy Rutherfurd's visits; she had heard

When the funeral train reached Washington, an army caisson drawn by six matched white horses took the coffin to the White House.

that Lucy had been with her husband when he died. Her daughter must have known of this; why had she not told her? Mother and daughter confronted each other tensely. Then, as always, Eleanor Roosevelt steadied herself. She returned to the East Room, had the casket opened, and dropped in some flowers. Then the casket was sealed for good. Later in the evening the funeral cortege went back to Union Station. Crowds still lined the avenues. The presidential train, with seventeen cars filled with officials and politicians, pulled out before midnight.

The train had brought Roosevelt's body up through Virginia, the land of Washington and Jefferson; now, from the capital all the way to Hyde Park, he would be following the route of Abraham Lincoln's last journey, and people would be thinking of the strange parallels between the two—the sudden, unbelievable deaths, the end for each coming in the final weeks of a terrible war, both in the month of April—and of things that seemed to be more than coincidence. Both men had been perplexing combinations of caution and courage, of practicality and principle; both had taken their countries into war after *faits accomplis* had allowed it; both had acted for black Americans only under great pressure.

Through the long night, under weeping clouds, the train moved north, through Baltimore to Wilmington to Philadelphia. And everywhere it was as it had been eighty years before:

> When lilacs last in the dooryard bloom'd . . .
> With the waiting depot, the arriving coffin,
>   and the sombre faces,
> With dirges through the night, with the
>   thousand voices rising strong and solemn . . .

That night, after the services, the coffin, attended by an honor guard, was put back on the train to carry Roosevelt home.

After all his delays and evasions Lincoln had won standing as a world hero, through emancipation and victory and martyrdom; but Roosevelt—what kind of hero was Roosevelt? Some close observers felt that people exaggerated Roosevelt's political courage. Clare Boothe Luce remarked that every great leader had his typical gesture—Hitler the upraised arm, Churchill the V sign. Roosevelt? She wet her index finger and held it up. Many others noted Roosevelt's cautiousness, even timidity. Instead of appealing to the people directly on great developing issues and taking clear and forthright action to anticipate emergencies, he typically allowed problems to fester and come to a head in the form of dramatic issues before acting with decision. He often took bold positions only to retreat from them in subsequent words or actions. He seemed unduly sensitive to both congressional and public opinion; he used public-opinion polls much more systematically than was realized at the time, even to the point one time of polling people on the question of who should succeed Frank Knox as Secretary of the Navy (Harold Stassen lost). His arresting speeches gave him a reputation as the fearless leader, but he spent far more time feinting and parrying in everyday politics than in mobilizing the country behind crucial decisions.

Around 2 A.M. the train crossed into New Jersey, the state where Woodrow Wilson had plunged into politics as a reformer, while young Roosevelt, impressed, watched from Hyde Park and Albany. Old Wilsonians later had compared Roosevelt unfavorably to the great idealist who had gone down fighting for his dream. Roosevelt, too, had watched that performance—had been part of it—and had drawn his conclusions from it. Robert Sherwood remembered him sitting at the end of the long table in the Cabinet room and looking up at the portrait of his onetime chief over the mantlepiece; the tragedy of Wilson, Sherwood said, was always somewhere within the rim of Roosevelt's consciousness.

"The tragedy of Wilson . . ." There were some who said that this was merely a personal tragedy for the man and a temporary tragedy for the nation and the world, that the prophetic warnings of the great crusader had been vindicated so dramatically by the collapse of the balance of power twenty years later, that Wilson's very defeat had made possible American commitment to a new international organization. Roosevelt did not share this view. He had no wish to be a martyr, to be vindicated only a generation later. He believed in moving on a wide, short front, pushing ahead here, retreating there, temporizing elsewhere, moving audaciously only when forces were leaning his way, so that one quick stroke—perhaps only a symbolic stroke, like a speech—would start in his direction the movement of press and public opinion, of Congress, his own administration, foreign peoples and governments. All this he could do only from a position of power, from the pulpit of the Presidency. To gain power meant winning elections; and to win elections required endless concessions to expediency and compromises with his own ideals.

Projected onto the international plane this strategy demanded of Roosevelt not only the usual expediency and opportunism but also a willingness to compromise with men and forces antagonistic to the ideals of Endicott Peabody and Woodrow Wilson. Again and again, self-consciously and indeed with bravado, he "walked with the devil" of the far right or far left, in his deals with France's Darlan and Italy's Badoglio, his toleration of Franco, his concessions to Stalin. Yet this self-confessed, if temporary, companion of Satan was also a Christian soldier striving for principles of democracy and freedom that he set forth with unsurpassed eloquence and persistence.

Did he then not "mean it"? So Roosevelt's enemies charged. It was all a trick, they said, to bamboozle the American people or their allies, to perpetuate himself in power, or to achieve some other sinister purpose. But it seems clear that Roosevelt did mean it, if meaning it is defined as intensity of personal conviction rooted in an ideological commitment. "Oh—he sometimes tries to appear tough and cynical and flippant, but that's an act he likes to put on, especially at press conferences," Harry Hopkins said to Sherwood. "He wants to make the boys think he's hardboiled. Maybe he fools some of them, now and then—but don't ever let him fool you, or you won't be any use to him. You can see the real Roosevelt when he comes out with something like the Four Freedoms. And don't get the idea that those are only catch phrases. *He believes them.* . . ."

Roosevelt, like Lincoln and Wilson, died fighting for his ideals. It might have been more dramatic if he had been assassinated by an ideological foe or had been stricken during a speech. But his decisions to aid Britain and Russia, his daring to take a position before the 1944 election against giving power to the Senate to sabotage America's peace-enforcing efforts in the proposed council of the United Nations, his long, exhausting trips to Tehran and Yalta, his patient efforts to win Stalin's personal friendship, his willingness to go out on a limb in his belief that the United States and the Soviet Union could work together in the postwar world—all this testified to the depth of his conviction.

Yet he could believe with equal conviction that his prime duty was to defend his nation's interests, safeguard its youth, win the war as quickly as possible, protect its postwar economy. With his unconquerable optimism he felt that he could do both things—pursue global ideals and national *Realpolitik*—simultaneously. So he tried to win Soviet friendship and confidence at the same time that he saved American lives by consenting to the delay in the cross-Channel invasion, thus letting the Red Army bleed. He paid tribute to the brotherly spirit of global science just before he died even while he was withholding atomic information from his partners the Russians. He wanted to unite liberal Democrats and internationalist Republicans in one progressive party, but he never did the spadework or took the personal political risks that such a strategy required. He yearned to help Indians and other Asiatic peoples gain their independence, but not at the risk of disrupting his military coalition with Britain and other Atlantic nations holding colonial possessions in Asia. He ardently hoped to bring a strong, united, and democratic China into the Big Four, but he refused to apply to Chungking the military resources and political pressure necessary to arrest the dry rot in that country. Above all, he wanted to build a

On April 15 the President's funeral train reached Hyde Park. A hooded, riderless horse, stirrups reversed and with sword and boots hanging upside down—symbol of a lost warrior—was led behind the coffin up the winding, gravelled road to the Roosevelt estate.

strong postwar international organization, but he dared not surrender his country's substantive veto in the proposed peace-keeping council, and as a practical matter he seemed more committed to Big Four, great-power peace-keeping than he did to a federation acting for the brotherhood of all mankind.

"I dream dreams but am, at the same time, an intensely practical person," Roosevelt wrote to Prime Minister Jan Christiaan Smuts of South Africa during the war. Both his dreams and his practicality were admirable; the problem lay in the relation between the two. He failed to work out the intermediary ends and means necessary to accomplish his purposes. Partly because of his disbelief in planning far ahead, partly because he elevated short-run goals over long-run, and always because of his experience and temperament, he did not fashion the structure of action, the full array of mutually consistent means—political, economic, psychological, military—necessary to realize his paramount ends.

So the more he preached his lofty ends and practiced his limited means, the more he reflected and encouraged the old habit of the American democracy to "praise the Lord—and keep your powder dry," and the more he widened the gap between popular expectations and actual possibilities. Not only did this derangement of ends and means lead to crushed hopes, disillusion, and cynicism at home, but it helped sow the seeds of the Cold War during World War II, as the Kremlin contrasted Roosevelt's coalition rhetoric with his Atlantic First strategy and falsely suspected a bourgeois conspiracy to destroy Soviet Communism. And Indians and Chinese contrasted Roosevelt's anticolonial words with his military concessions to colonial powers and falsely inferred that he was an imperialist at heart and a hypocrite to boot.

Roosevelt's critics attacked him as naïve, ignorant, amateurish, in foreign affairs, but this man who had bested all his domestic enemies and most of his foreign ones was no innocent. His supreme difficulty lay not in his views as to what *was*—he had a Shakespearean appreciation of all the failings, vices, cruelties, and complexities of man—but of what *could be*. The last words he ever wrote, on the eve of his death, were the truest words he ever wrote. He had a strong and active faith, a huge and unprovable faith, in the possibilities of human understanding, trust, and love. He could say with the theologian Reinhold Niebuhr that love is the law of life even when people do not live by the law of love.

It was still dark when the train drew into Pennsylvania Station. New York had been alive with rumors that Jack Dempsey or Frank Sinatra or some other celebrity had died, too. At the time of Roosevelt's funeral service in the White House, New York City news presses stopped rolling, radios went silent, subway trains came

to a halt, police held up traffic. In Carnegie Hall the Boston Symphony Orchestra, under Serge Koussevitzky, played Beethoven's *Eroica* symphony. Roosevelt's train paused for a time at the Mott Haven railroad yards in the Bronx, then moved up the east bank of the Hudson—the route that Roosevelt had taken so often before.

Newspapers were still reporting people's reactions around the world—still reporting the shock, incredulity, and fear, but above all the sense of having lost a friend. In Moscow, black-bordered flags flew at half mast; Soviet newspapers, which invariably printed foreign news on the back page, published the news of Roosevelt's death and his picture on page one. The theme of the editorials in Russia was friendship. Many Russians were seen weeping in the street. The *Court Circular* of Buckingham Palace broke ancient precedent by reporting the death of a chief of state not related to the British ruling family; Roosevelt would have been pleased. In Chungking a coolie read the wall newspapers, newly wet with shiny black ink, and turned away muttering, "*Tai tsamsso liao*" ("It was too soon that he died"). "Your President is dead," an Indian said to a passing G.I., "a friend of poor. . . ." Everywhere, noted Anne O'Hare McCormick, the refrain was, "We have lost a friend."

It was this enormous fund of friendship on which Roosevelt expected to draw in carrying out his hopes for the postwar world. He expected to combine his friendships with captains and kings and his standing with masses of people with his political skills and America's resources to strengthen the United Nations, maintain good relations with the Soviets, help the Chinese realize the Four Freedoms, and discourage European colonialism in Asia and Africa. But all depended on his being on deck, being in the White House.

The train threaded its way along the curving tracks on the bank of the Hudson, passing the towering Palisades across the river—High Tor, Sugarloaf, Storm King. At Garrison, opposite West Point, men removed their hats just as they had done eighty years before. Then Cold Spring, Beacon, Poughkeepsie, on the bank of the Hudson, the river of American politics.

Around the world men who had known Roosevelt were struggling to phrase their eulogies. Churchill was preparing a tribute for Parliament, but he would say nothing more cogent than his Tehran toast to Roosevelt as a leader who had "guided his country along the tumultuous stream of party friction and internal politics amidst the violent freedom of democracy." The Russian diplomat Ivan Maisky would remember him as a statesman of very great calibre, with an acute mind, a wide sweep in action, vast energy, but in the end essentially bourgeois, flesh of the flesh of the American ruling class. John Buchan, author and Canadian governor general, felt that he had never met a man more fecund in ideas;

BOTH: BROWN BROTHERS

WIDE WORLD

Burial was in the rose garden. Above left, Fala, the President's Scottie, strained at the leash as the coffin moved past him. Center, Mrs. Roosevelt stood with impeccable dignity throughout the service. Afterward she was escorted away by her son Elliott, who carried the flag that had draped the coffin. Anna Boettiger was with her mother, and beyond her stood Harry Truman.

Robert Sherwood found him spiritually the healthiest man he had ever known; Henry Stimson called him an ideal wartime commander in chief, the greatest war President the nation had ever had. Young Congressman Lyndon Johnson, grieving over the news of the death of his friend, said Roosevelt was the only person he had ever known who was never afraid. "God, how he could take it for us all!"

A second-rate intellect, Oliver Wendell Holmes had called him, but a first-rate temperament. To examine closely single aspects of Roosevelt's character—as thinker, as organizer, as manipulator, as strategist, as idealist—is to see failings and deficiencies interwoven with the huge capacities. But to stand back and look at the man as a whole, against the backdrop of his people and his times, is to see the lineaments of greatness—courage, joyousness, responsiveness, vitality, faith. A democrat in manner and conviction, he was yet a member of that small aristocracy once described by E. M. Forster: sensitive but not weak, considerate but not fussy, plucky in his power to endure, capable of laughing and of taking a joke. He was the true happy warrior.

"All that is within me cries out to go back to my home on the Hudson River," Roosevelt had said nine months before. The train, still hugging the riverbank, moved from Poughkeepsie into Hyde Park. It was Sunday, April 15, 1945, a clear day, the sky a deep blue. Tiny waves were breaking against the river shore where the train slowed and switched off onto a siding below the bluff on which the mansion stood. Cannon sounded twenty-one times as the coffin was moved from the train to a caisson drawn by six brown horses. Standing behind was a seventh horse, hooded, stirrups reversed, sword and boots turned upside down hanging from the left stirrup—symbolic of a lost warrior.

Following the beat of muffled drums, the little procession toiled up the steep, winding, gravelled road, past a small stream running full and fast, past the ice pond, with its surface a smoky jade under the overhanging hemlocks, past the budding apple trees and the lilacs and the open field, and emerged onto the height. In back of the house, standing in the rose garden framed by the hemlock hedge, was a large assembly: President Truman and his Cabinet, the officialdom of the old administration, family and friends and retainers, and a phalanx of six hundred West Point cadets standing rigidly at attention in their gray uniforms and white crossed belts. Behind the coffin, borne now by eight servicemen, Eleanor Roosevelt and her daughter, Anna, and her son Elliott moved into the rose garden.

The aged rector of St. James Episcopal Church of Hyde Park prayed, ". . . earth to earth, ashes to ashes, dust to dust." Raising his hand as the servicemen lowered the body slowly into the grave, he intoned:

> *Now the laborer's task is o'er,*
> *Now the battle day is past,*
> *Now upon the farther shore*
> *Lands the voyager at last. . . .*

A breeze off the Hudson ruffled the trees above. Cadets fired three volleys. A bugler played the haunting notes of taps. The soldier was home.

The Thankless Task of Nicholas Trist CONTINUED FROM PAGE 15

ing him of its contents, Trist chose to remain at Vera-cruz and to write a letter to the General in which he requested that the sealed dispatch be delivered to the Mexican minister of foreign affairs. With this communication he enclosed one from William L. Marcy, the Secretary of War, which ordered Scott to transmit the sealed letter to the Mexicans and informed him that "Mr. Trist, an officer from our department of foreign affairs, next in rank to its chief," was now at Army headquarters.

Scott exploded. Under the best of circumstances he was a proud man, excruciatingly sensitive of his reputation and quick to detect a slight whether or not one was intended. Temperament aside, there was also the fact that he was a prominent Whig—a political foe of the administration in Washington—and had long since fallen out with President Polk. In fact, at the time Polk gave Scott command of the Army in May, 1846, the tactless General had written the President an offensive letter complaining about Democratic place-seekers and then had confided to Secretary of War Marcy that he had no stomach for placing himself "in the most perilous of all positions:—a fire upon my rear, from Washington, and the fire in the front, from the Mexicans." Polk's furious reaction had been to excuse Scott from field command in Mexico, leaving him to stew in the capital while Zachary Taylor won the victories and the glory. Finally, in November, 1846, Scott was sent to command the movement on Veracruz and Mexico City, but Polk neither forgave nor forgot. He wrote in his diary:

General Scott has acted with so little discretion since he assumed the command that the confidential plans of the Government which were confided only to himself have been made so public that every Mexican may know them. . . . His vanity is such that he could not keep the most important secrets of the Government which were given to him. He is . . . making such a parade before the public in all he does that there is danger that the objects of the campaign may be entirely defeated. . . .

Such a background was not one to make Scott warm to Trist, and what was to have been a co-operative mission between the two was immediately thrown into jeopardy. Still in the dark about the contents of the proposed treaty, Scott wrote an outraged answer to Trist's first letter. It began: "I see that the secretary of War proposes to degrade me, requiring that I, as commander-in-chief of this army, shall defer to you, the chief clerk in the Dep't of State, the question of continuing or discontinuing hostilities." After getting that out of his system, he indicated that since there was no real Mexican government, he could not forward the dispatch anyway.

Here Nicholas Trist, had he had his wits about him, would have recognized his initial error and attempted to patch things up with the General. But no, he sent off one of his endless communications—an eighteen-page letter that Scott termed "sarcastic, burning, and impo-

Winfield Scott, the American Commander in Chief, turned from Trist's most difficult opponent into one of his staunchest supporters. Here he reviews victorious troops in Mexico City.

lite." By now Polk's peace mission was completely off the rails. Scott, assuming Trist to be an ally of Polk and Buchanan (both of whom he mistrusted because they had opposed his appointment as commanding general), now believed that the government in Washington was deliberately trying to prevent him from having a voice in a truce with the Mexicans. Trist, no less suspicious, wrote his wife that Scott was "decidedly the greatest imbecile that I have ever had anything to do with" and soon was exchanging further angry letters with him. By May 29—more than three weeks after Trist arrived to negotiate a peace with the Mexican government—he had still not even met the U.S. Commander in Chief, who wrote him a curt note referring to one of Trist's thirty-page onslaughts as a "farrago of impudence, conceit, and arrogance."

Fortunately for posterity, both men were now being taken to task by their chiefs: Buchanan wrote Trist telling him that this was no time for a personal vendetta—the government, he said, could not indulge its representatives in a quarrel; Marcy told off Scott in similar fashion. Despite their differences and their abraded nerve ends, both men were good Americans, and they soon realized how detrimental to the nation's interests their conduct was. Nicholas Trist took the initial step to heal the rift: on June 25 he sent Scott a note that was for the first time free of rancor, and Scott replied at once, saying that he would be quite willing to forget the recent unpleasantness. Just then Trist fell ill, causing Scott to feel more compassionate toward him; on July 6 a box of guava marmalade was delivered to the diplomat's sickbed from the Commander in Chief, and with this peace offering the feud ended as suddenly as it had begun. A few days later the two met for the first time and established an immediate *entente cordiale;* soon contrite letters were on their way to Washington from both of them to their respective departments, requesting that the earlier, angry letters of complaint be removed from the files.

But by this time, naturally enough, the President of the United States was thoroughly disgusted with both his representatives. In addition to what he knew from other sources of the Trist-Scott feud, he had been receiving confidential dispatches from Scott's second-in-command, General Gideon J. Pillow, Polk's former law partner in Tennessee, who lost no opportunity to put Scott (and, after the *rapprochement*, Trist) in the worst possible light. Pillow was no fool; he wanted the top job himself, and thanks in part to his machinations, Polk gave renewed consideration to removing Scott from command.

Because of the horrendous delays in getting word from the battlefield to Washington—it often took three or four weeks for a message to reach the capital—there was an Alice-in-Wonderland aspect to the whole affair by this time, so that while Polk fumed at the White House over the lack of progress, events in Mexico were actually pushing matters toward a settlement. In August, Trist met for the first time with the Mexican peace commissioners, who balked at parting with Texas south of the Nueces River and a portion of Upper California. Since the Rio Grande boundary was a *sine qua non* of Trist's instructions, he broke off the talks; but he agreed to submit the Mexican proposal to Washington. Meanwhile the course of the war made peace inevitable: on September 14 the Americans captured Mexico City, Santa Anna and the government fled, and Trist observed that "total dissolution" of the country was at hand. In this state

of chaos Mexico would neither negotiate nor fight.

But as far as Washington knew, the unpopular war was merely dragging on, and President Polk could take no comfort from the fact that his Democrats were outnumbered in the House 117 to 110. Having heard further from Pillow that Trist was "acting unwisely," he concluded that no good could possibly come of the peace mission and told the Secretary of State to order his "commissioner plenipotentiary" to return home. So on October 6 Buchanan, unaware that Mexico City had fallen, wrote Trist telling him how conditions had changed since the previous April, reminding him of the American lives and treasure that had been squandered since then, and informing him, finally, that he was recalled. If Trist had written a treaty by the time he received these instructions, the Secretary added, he should of course bring it home with him; but if not, he should not delay his departure even though he might be in the midst of negotiations with the Mexicans. The next day, probably out of friendship and to soften the blow of Trist's recall, Buchanan followed up his official letter with a chatty personal note telling his friend how much he looked forward to having him back in the department again.

Two weeks later—on October 21—letters Trist had written on September 28 were received in Washington, making it clear that he had discussed terms with the Mexicans that exceeded his carefully drafted instructions. That was too much for Polk: his commissioner had "embarrassed future negotiations," the President spluttered. His conduct was "much to be regretted," since he had evidently encouraged the Mexicans to hope for better conditions than he had any right to promise them.

In November, when Trist finally received his letter of recall, along with other letters criticizing his actions, he characteristically sat down and wrote a lengthy justification of his conduct during the negotiations. Time and events certainly seemed to support Trist's hopes that a settlement would be reached before long. He was convinced that the Mexican peace party would form a government; Santa Anna, the defeated leader, had resigned the presidency, and the army had not rallied to him when he fled the Mexican capital. He had been succeeded by Manuel de la Peña y Peña, the president of the supreme court, who appointed a peace advocate as his minister of relations. But just at that moment, with the Mexicans on the verge of peace talks, Trist's recall had arrived. To his wife he wrote of his bitter disappointment; he intended to resign from the State Department, he told her, and "bid adieu *forever* to official life." Over and above his personal chagrin he could not understand why his government—if it sincerely desired peace, as he assumed—did not replace him with another peace commissioner. On December 1, when no word of a replacement had reached him, Trist decided to ignore his recall and stay in Mexico to write a treaty. He had concluded that he could not permit the present opportunity to slip by, and on December 6 he wrote to inform Buchanan of his decision. Even if new commissioners were appointed now, he argued, they could not arrive in time to salvage the situation, and if the opportunity were lost now, it might be gone forever. As for the boundaries, he realized that those limits included in his original instructions were the maximum to which the Mexicans could agree. With great sensitivity Trist wrote, "however helpless a nation may feel, there is necessarily a point beyond which she cannot be expected to go under any circumstances, in surrendering her territory as the price of peace."

One hopes that President Polk was spared the full catalogue of Trist's arguments, since his letter ran to sixty-five pages, but in any event Polk reacted predictably. He ordered Trist out of Army headquarters at once and instructed the United States military commander to inform the Mexicans that Nicholas P. Trist was no longer acting for the United States government. Separately, the President had also decided to replace Scott, having heard from Pillow and other subordinate officers that Scott was taking all the credit for victory over the Mexicans. (Robert E. Lee, a young colonel who had participated in that victory, wrote sadly to a friend concerning the dissensions in the Army. "No one can regret them more than I do. They have clouded a bright campaign. . . . The affair I suppose will soon be before the court . . . but I suspect that if one party [Scott] has been guilty of harshness . . . the other [Pillow and other dissident officers] has been guilty of insubordination.")

Trist responded to adversity by writing still more letters, assuring Buchanan that it was not personal vanity but devotion to duty that prompted him to remain in Mexico. Since he had not been replaced, he repeated, he would stay and achieve a peaceful settlement out of regard for both nations. At long last, on December 30, 1847, peace negotiations began in the town of Guadalupe Hidalgo, outside Mexico City. Trist was handicapped by having not even a secretary to assist him, so he was obliged to keep minutes while listening to the Mexican proposals. Each night he retired to write voluminous letters to Buchanan and to his wife.

On January 25 he was able to inform the Secretary of State that the terms of a treaty had been agreed upon. He had obtained the boundaries called for in his original instructions with only a slight variation at the western extremity; but he believed that the new line, which included the fine port of San Diego, fulfilled his orders in principle, and it was acceptable to the Mexicans. The defeated government was to be paid an indemnity of $15,000,000 for the territory taken by the United States,

and the victors were to assume claims against Mexico up to $3,250,000. On his own hook, Trist had worked out a solution to the status of Mexicans living in the ceded lands. If they elected to move out of what was now U.S. territory, they could take their belongings with them, without penalty; if they decided to remain, they could retain their Mexican citizenship provided that within a year they announced their intention to do so—otherwise they would become U.S. citizens.

On February 2, 1848, after a rash of delays caused by the Mexican commissioners, Trist wrote proudly to Buchanan informing him that the Treaty of Peace, Friendship, Limits, and Settlement had been signed that day at Guadalupe Hidalgo. Since Trist now had to remain in Mexico to testify at a court of inquiry ordered by President Polk to examine the charges brought by several members of Scott's staff concerning the conduct of the war, he asked James L. Freaner, correspondent for the New Orleans *Delta*, to carry the treaty back to the United States. As Robert Arthur Brent has written, the completed treaty was the most important achievement of Trist's life. If Trist had acted "at times negligently, at others without tact," he had nonetheless never lost sight of his objective, which was the establishing of peace between Mexico and the United States. "His success," Brent adds, "was the glory of the Polk administration; his disgrace was his own to bear."

And the signs all pointed to disgrace now. When Buchanan brought the treaty to Polk at the White House on February 19, the President was still angry over Trist's behavior, although he was forced to admit that the document met all the conditions given to Trist in April, 1847. After thinking the matter over, Polk informed his Cabinet that he would submit the treaty to the Senate. If he did not do so, he reasoned, Congress might react by refusing to appropriate money to keep the Army in Mexico, and Polk would have to withdraw the troops without a peace treaty. The Whigs who had attacked the war so bitterly would surely make political capital out of his failure to end it, especially when the treaty embodied the very terms laid down by Polk himself. And finally, Polk was keenly aware of the immense value of the lands ceded by this treaty to the United States. So on February 23—against the advice of Buchanan, who wanted to demand even more territory from the defeated Mexicans —Polk sent the treaty to the Senate, including with it a remarkable note recommending that it be debated on its own merits and without reference to the unfortunate actions of Nicholas P. Trist. The Senate responded by requesting from the President all correspondence relating to Trist's mission, and members of the Foreign Relations Committee informed Polk that they would recommend rejection—not because of the terms of the treaty but because Trist had written it after his recall.

Polk fought back at once. The senators were usurping the powers of the Chief Executive, he stated firmly; the Senate might consider the treaty itself, but not how it had been made—that was the prerogative of the President. There was formidable opposition to the treaty: Thomas Hart Benton led a group of Democrats who opposed ratification on moral grounds—the United States, they said, had no right to any territory other than Texas south to the Nueces River; Daniel Webster, leading the Whig forces, opposed it on the basis that the United States would thereby acquire too much territory; and another group of Democrats was against it because the United States did not get *enough* land. But on March 10, with four senators not voting, the treaty was finally approved by a vote of thirty-eight to fourteen.

And what of the treaty's chief advocate? Poor Trist, after wrangling with Army authorities over his right as an American citizen to remain in Mexico, was placed under arrest as the only means of getting him to leave the country where he had toiled for so long. When he rejoined his family in Washington at last, on May 17, 1848, thirteen months had elapsed since his departure, and he found himself dismissed from government service in disgrace. Buchanan, now completely out of favor with the President, could not help him. (Polk had grown increasingly suspicious of his Secretary of State because of his presidential aspirations: "No candidate for the presidency ought ever to remain in the Cabinet," Polk noted in his diary. "He is an unsafe adviser.") And the President, of course, wanted nothing to do with Trist. Although Trist, more than any other man, was responsible for fulfilling Polk's ambition of rounding out the natural boundaries of the United States, the President could not bring himself to forgive his act of disobedience. Indeed, since Trist had been on a secret mission and therefore was paid out of the President's special funds, he was even denied his full pay by the Chief Executive, who cut off his salary as of November 16, when he received his recall.

In a memorial to Congress, Trist pleaded his cause: he had not sought the appointment as peace commissioner; he had been asked to render a great service to his country; in doing so, he had saved thousands of lives and millions of dollars; he had acquired a vast territory for the United States, extending our western boundary to the Pacific and fixing firm boundaries between Mexico and the United States where none had existed. Surely a man who had achieved that deserved recognition? But the Congress was not in a forgiving mood either.

Virtually destitute, Trist and his wife moved to West Chester, Pennsylvania, in July of 1848. Fortunately, a few friends—Winfield Scott among them—offered him help. During his stay there several writers came to him

in search of information about the great men he had known: Henry S. Randall, for his biography of Jefferson; James Parton, for his biography of Jackson; Thomas Hart Benton, for assistance on his *Thirty Years' View*. By 1855, with his wife running a school for young ladies, Nicholas Trist was reduced to taking a job as a clerk for the Wilmington and Baltimore Railroad Company, where he eventually worked up to paymaster at a salary of $112.50 a month. It was a bitter lot for a man who had been so close to the nation's great and had done so much for his country.

As the Civil War approached, Trist was drawn again to politics—for the New York *World* he wrote an article quoting Jefferson's and Madison's views on secession. To General Scott, a Virginian who was now commanding general of the Union Army, he wrote that he was also a southerner by birth and a Yankee by adoption, but that his sympathies and those of his wife lay with the North and with preservation of the Union. Now and again Trist's friends tried to help him obtain a government job. In 1861 Scott wrote to the Secretary of the Treasury, Salmon P. Chase, stating that Trist had been wronged by Polk and neglected by Taylor, Fillmore, Pierce, and Buchanan; the nation owed Nicholas Trist a great debt, the old soldier added. But Chase did nothing. Finally, in 1870, Senator Charles Sumner made an eloquent speech in Trist's behalf, reminding the Senate of his signal contributions, and a year later Trist received the sum of $14,559.90—money that was owed him for his salary and expenses in Mexico twenty-three years earlier. It came none too soon, for he had had to give up his railway job a year earlier, and the Trists were poverty-stricken. In the summer of 1870 President Grant appointed him postmaster in Alexandria, Virginia. He was paid $2,900 a year, which was more money than he had earned at any time since 1841, but he had less than four years to enjoy this munificence. On February 11, 1874, after suffering a stroke, Trist died.

Anyone wishing to contemplate the part chance plays in human destiny might give some thought to the career of Nicholas P. Trist. His act of rare courage and principle for a cause he believed to be right cost him the support of the President and brought him dismissal, disgrace, poverty, and the total disregard of posterity. Most historians have neglected him entirely or dismissed him as a man of no ability, overlooking the fact that Trist was a victim of an unpopular war and an administration that neither understood nor sympathized with his difficulties or his aspirations. Immovable on matters of principle, Trist determined to do what he considered right. And for this, as well as for the tangible effects of his deed, he deserves better of his country.

What the nation obtained as a result of the treaty he executed singlehandedly was the boundary of the Rio

Grande and the cession of territory between that river and the Pacific Ocean—which includes the present states of California, Nevada, Utah, New Mexico, Arizona, a corner of Wyoming, and the western slope of Colorado. Because of the efforts of Nicholas P. Trist, James K. Polk is remembered as the President who, except for Jefferson, added more territory to the nation that any other. When Polk left office the United States was half again as large as when he took the oath. As a final irony, while Nicholas P. Trist and the Mexicans were reaching final agreement in Guadalupe Hidalgo, gold was discovered at Sutter's Mill in California, with consequences beyond all imagining.

Mr. Ketchum, Senior Editor for Book Publishing of American Heritage Publishing Company, is the author of the "Faces from the Past" series that has appeared frequently in this magazine. These pieces, together with many new ones, will be published soon in book form under the same title by American Heritage Press.

Among the sources for this article were: "Nicholas Philip Trist: Biography of a Disobedient Diplomat," an unpublished doctoral dissertation written in 1950 by Robert Arthur Brent at the University of Virginia, and "Nicholas P. Trist, a Diplomat with Ideals," an article in the Mississippi Valley Historical Review *for June, 1924, by Louis M. Sears. A good over-all view of the period is in* The War with Mexico, *by Justin H. Smith (two volumes, Macmillan, 1919).*

"Rebels, turn out your dead!" CONTINUED FROM PAGE 17

ings, keelhaulings, iron shackles, and starvation rations were accepted instruments of enforcing discipline. Despite the understandably angry indictments of a score or more survivors who left long memoirs of the miseries they suffered aboard H.M.S. *Jersey*, the British were neither more nor less severe as captors than any civilized nation of that era.

In the case of the maritime prisoners of the Revolution, there was also calculation rather than malice behind the rough treatment. The most valued commodity to the British Navy was manpower for its great fleet of ships. Navy service was not very appealing. Voyages lasted months on end, and shipboard life was demanding, cramped, and sustained with little more than a bare survival diet. Death and disappearance were commonplace, and the records of every maritime family abounded with the sad notation, "Lost at sea." Efforts to recruit a ship's crew ranged from boisterous parties, staged primarily to get prospects sufficiently drunk so that when they woke up they were well out to sea, to actual impressment, a euphemism for outright kidnapping at the point of a pistol or the edge of a cutlass.

Under these circumstances tempting sources of manpower for British ships were the crews of captured Yankee vessels. They were, on the whole, well-trained, experienced seamen. They spoke English. And as far as the British were concerned, they were, though in rebellion, still British subjects. Furthermore, since the colonists assigned a major burden of their naval activities to privateers, few of the American captives were technically prisoners of war, and the British felt that they should be treated merely as private seamen committing crimes on the high seas. It was their hope that the prisoners would find life aboard the prison ships so intolerable that they would gladly enlist in His Majesty's service. Some

did, planning, in many cases, to desert the enemy's forces later.

Far more often, however, whether from loyalty to the American cause or from sheer stubbornness, the prisoners endured the harrowing routine of boredom, hunger, disease, bitter cold or sweltering heat, and imminence of death that constituted life aboard *Jersey*. More than eleven hundred men were crammed between decks at night without cots or hammocks, and so crowded was her spar deck by day that they had to take turns walking in platoons along narrow aisles kept open for that purpose. Night was the most horrible time. At sundown the guards bellowed, "Down, rebels, down!" and the half-naked, emaciated men descended through narrow hatchways, each of which was guarded by a solitary sentry once the grating covers were in place. The only concession to naval amenities was made by the prisoners themselves, who agreed that their officers should have the former gun room, aft on the middle deck, to themselves.

The dreaded nightly routine on *Jersey* was graphically recalled by Christopher Hawkins, who was captured in 1781 when the Providence brig *Mariamne*, five days out of Newport, was taken by two British frigates:

We were all put between decks ev'ry night before dark, the number being great our situation was here extremely unpleasant. . . . Although the british had an hospital ship near us for the accommodation of the sick yet we had a great deal of sickness on board the Jersey, and many died on board her. The sickness seemed to be epidemic and which we called the bloody flux or dyssenterry. After the prisoners had been driven below at dusk of the evening and the boat had ceased conveying the sick to the hospital ship, many of the prisoners would become sick the fore part of the evening and before morning their suffering would be ended by death—such was the malignancy of the disease. My situation amongst others after being stowed away for the night was on the larboard side of the ship with our heads near the wall or side, and the two boys before mentioned [brothers who had been cooks on *Mariamne*] by the side of me. Thus situated, but one gangway to the upper deck was open, from which my place of rest was about 20 feet, and only two prisoners were allowed to visit the upper deck at the same time in the night let the calls of nature be never so violent, and there was no place between decks provided us to satisfy those calls. This induced an almost constant running over me by the sick, who would besmear myself and others with their bloody and loathsome filth.

Death in the night was a common occurrence in *Jersey*'s steaming hull in the summer and equally so in the cold of the long winter. Six to eleven men died every twenty-four hours, largely from dysentery, smallpox, typhoid, and yellow fever. Routinely the first morning call of the sentry was "Rebels, turn out your dead!" The corpses were carried up the hatchways to the main deck, sewn into their blankets if they had any, lowered into the ship's boat, and taken ashore to where a hill sloped down from Remsen's barn to the tidal shore. There, on a thin neck of land between a millpond and the bay, they were buried by shipmates, under armed guard, in shallow mass graves. Duty on these burial parties was desperately sought—solely to get away, however briefly, from the omnipresent stench of the ship and to set foot for a few precious minutes on land. "It was a high gratification," Dring remembered, "to us to bury our feet in the sand, and to shove them through it, as we passed on our way. We went by a small patch of turf, some pieces of which we tore up from the earth; and [we] obtained permission to carry them on board, for our comrades to smell them." The makeshift graves were far from adequate, and at every flood tide scores of bodies were washed loose—a fact that haunted the men of the burial parties the rest of their lives. "They [the guards] scarcely allowed us time to look about us," Dring continued, "for no sooner had we heaped the earth above the trench than the order was given to march. But a single glance was sufficient to show us parts of many bodies which were exposed to view; although they had probably been placed there, with the same mockery of interment, but a few days before."

Jeremiah Johnson, a teen-age farm boy who lived next to the Remsens, never forgot the gruesome burial grounds. "The whole shore, from Rennie's Point, to Mr. Remsen's dooryard," he wrote, "was a place of graves; as were also the slope of the hill near the house; the shore, from Mr. Remsen's barn along the mill-pond to Rappelye's farm. . . . The atmosphere seemed to be charged with foul air from the prison ships and with the effluvia of dead bodies washed out of their graves by the tides. . . . The bodies of the dead lay exposed along the beach, drying and bleaching in the sun, and whitening the shores."

Despite the constant spectre of sickness and death, the prisoners did what they could to maintain order among themselves, to make the most of their pitiable rations, and to increase their chances of survival. Dysentery and malaria were hard to cope with, but the prisoners used to inoculate themselves against smallpox, most prevalent and deadly of their afflictions, by using a common pin to scarify the skin, usually on the hand, and applying to the raw spot some discharge taken from the lesion of an infected shipmate. The able-bodied were organized into working parties who, in return for scrubbing the decks and hoisting supplies aboard, were given extra rations and "the privilege of going on deck, early in the morning, to breathe the pure air." Among the less fortunate, codes of conduct were voluntarily promulgated among the prisoners, largely directed at preserving whatever health remained by enforcing rather elementary sanitary rules and at preventing "immorality," ranging from the use of profane language to theft and assault.

Particular attention was given to the equitable distribution of food. This consisted, according to Andrew Sherburne, the captured boatswain of the Maine brig *Scorpion*, "of worm eaten bread, and salt beef. It was supposed that this bread and beef had been condemned in the British navy. The bread had been so eaten by weevils, that one might easily crush it in the hand and blow it away. The beef was exceedingly salt, and scarcely a particle of fat could be seen on it." The beef was boiled in dirty sea water that was drawn up from the side of the ship where the wastes of over a thousand men were dumped daily.

Forbidding as the food was, the prisoners treated their scanty, nauseous rations with respect and fanatical discipline. Ebenezer Fox told how the prisoners were divided into small parties, or "messes," of six men each, for the purpose of obtaining and distributing their food. "The persons chosen by each mess . . . were summoned by the cook's bell to receive their allowance, and, when it had remained in the boiler a certain time, the bell would again sound, and the allowance must be immediately taken away: whether it was sufficiently cooked or not, it could remain no longer." The unsavory diet of the prisoners was occasionally relieved by bran stolen from the troughs of hogs kept in pens on the gun deck as pork for the ship's officers' mess. Sometimes, in the summer, nearby farmers would send vegetables to the ship. A fat old woman known as Dame Grant came alongside every other day in a small boat rowed by two boys, and peddled sugar, tea, and other small supplies to those who had some currency. But this did not last long. Dame Grant contracted a fever from the prisoners and died, leaving no successor.

With food so scarce, the prisoners naturally took a very stern view of anyone among them who cheated in the distribution system. As Christopher Hawkins reported:

A prisoner had pilfered food from a mess, who complained of him to the chief british officer on board. This officer decided that the delinquent should be punished by all the members of the mess who had suffered by his pillage. The accused was tied across a water butt [cask] on the upper deck—his posteriors were laid bare, and a wooden instrument six feet long, one end expanded and shaped much in the form of an oar [was brought out] . . . The mess-mates who had suffered by his pilfering, and six in number were arranged around him . . . Next, one of the mess took the instrument in hand (it was very heavy, and as much so as one man could conveniently wield)—and inflicted six strokes with the ponderous weapon, apparently with all his might—the sufferer groaning at every stroke—blood

John Trumbull, the famous artist of the Revolution, called this drawing "Prisoners Starving to Death." On Jersey *they were more likely to die of pestilence, although the food was horrid.*

appeared before the first six were administered—a second man took the instrument and with no less mercy than the first inflicted six more strokes—the blood and flesh flying ten feet at ev'ry stroke—during this period the defaulter fainted, but was resuscitated by administering water to him—a third man took the instrument in hand and inflicted six more strokes though not as severe as the first—The officer before mentioned then interposed and observed to the enraged mess-mates that they were too severe with their fellow. He had again fainted. No more blows were given and the horrible looking man was untied and fell down on the deck. He was again resuscitated but still lay prostrated on the deck, not being able to rise. Beef brine was thrown upon his wounds but he appeared to be senseless. . . . The sufferer died in two or three days after his punishment. . . .

The code of the prisoners was obviously tough and uncompromising but, when weighed against their common plight, not unjust. Nor was it, at a time when the cat-o'-

nine-tails was often applied for very simple shipboard offences, exceptionally harsh or sadistic. The men who took to the sea were hard men, whose conduct was based on simplistic copybook maxims; if they were relentless in their application of these, they were also consistent and knew what to expect of one another. In the primitive conditions aboard a prison ship such elemental standards of honor were important. Escape, for example, was—next to death—the most common method of a prisoner's leaving *Jersey*. Yet the realities of confinement made it virtually impossible for a man to plot or execute an escape without his shipmates knowing about it. Moreover, once ashore, he had to get through the British-held stretches of Long Island—all of it Tory country, where the American hatred of rebels equalled the British—and thence across the Sound to the mainland well beyond the British outposts of New York City.

To reduce risks and to furnish mutual help, most escapes from *Jersey* were group ventures. For this reason informers were treated with thorough contempt and deadly retaliation. As Thomas Andros, who was interned on *Jersey* in 1781, recalled:

A secret, prejudicial to a prisoner, revealed to the guard, was death. Captain Young of Boston, concealed himself in a large chest belonging to a sailor going to be exchanged, and was carried on board the cartel [a ship sailing under safe conduct for such purposes as to convey messages between belligerents or to exchange prisoners], and we considered his escape as certain; but the secret leaked out and he was brought back, and one Spicer of Providence, being suspected as the traitor, the enraged prisoners were about to take his life. His head was drawn back, and the knife raised to cut his throat, but having obtained a hint of what was going on below, the guard at this instant, rushed down and rescued the man.

If Christopher Hawkins is to be believed, Spicer, a sailing master's mate, was incorrigible. Hawkins reported that a cabin boy was smuggled onto an exchange ship in a sea chest and "the treacherous Spicer communicated the affair to the commanding officer of the prison ship. The cartel was immediately boarded, as she had not yet left the port, although ready to leave, and the boy found and brought back. Spicer paid for his treachery with the forfeit of his life—When evening was coming on, and the prisoners were going below for the night, he was knocked down the hatchway to the bottom of the steps below among those who had been awaiting his fall, and who fell upon him, cut off his ears and mangled his body in the most shocking manner, and to such a degree that he died of his wounds in a day or two after."

Since escape from *Jersey*, when not frustrated by informers, was often successful, the possibility of mutiny must have occurred to new prisoners. There were sometimes as many as fourteen hundred prisoners aboard, and the crew of the ship consisted of only seventeen men

—a commander, two mates, a steward, a cook, and twelve sailors; the armed guard consisted of from twelve to forty somewhat tired functionaries, variously made up of invalid marines, English troops detached from duty in regiments stationed on Long Island, Hessians, or refugee American loyalists. (These last were worst of all because of their efforts to prove themselves more loyal than the king.) Even in their decrepit condition the prisoners could easily have overpowered His Majesty's representatives. It might have been difficult at night, when the prisoners were below decks and one guard with a gun and fixed bayonet could control a hatchway (although Ebenezer Fox reported that one sentinel at a main hatchway, a tough Irishman called "Billy the Ram," "while leaning carelessly on his gun" and talking with a prisoner, "received a tremendous blow from the fist of his entertainer, on the back of his head, which brought him to the deck in a state of insensibility," and permitted the escape of fifteen of the thirty men who reached the upper decks). But in daytime, when the mass of prisoners was swarming on the upper deck and a guard would not have had room to aim a gun or raise a bayonet, the guards and the entire crew could have been thrown overboard.

Why, then, was there no mutiny? The answer lay in the weakened condition of the prisoners. Half-starved and sick, they would have severely tested their remaining energy just getting to shore. Then, without supplies or transportation, they would have had to travel through miles and miles of enemy-held territory and enemy-controlled waters. Under these circumstances, mutiny would have amounted ultimately to little more than mass suicide.

If mutiny was out of the question, so was any prospect of a mass exchange. No one on the colonial side seemed to have any effective authority to deal with privateer seamen held by the enemy. Had such authority existed, the colonials were in a very poor bargaining position, since none of the colonies wanted the expense of imprisoning captured British sailors (they just let them go or enlisted them on their own ships), and, as a result, had no one to exchange. As for the few official American naval prisoners aboard *Jersey*, it was the policy of the British to offer in exchange only those prisoners who had been incarcerated so long that their capacity for service was all but extinct and their early death almost inevitable.

General Washington had no authority over either naval or privateer prisoners, but in any case he opposed exchanging American seamen, particularly privateersmen, for British soldiers because, as he wrote the President of the Continental Congress, it "will immediately give the enemy a very considerable re-enforcement, and will be a constant draft hereafter upon the prisoners of war in our hands. It ought also to be considered that few or none of the naval prisoners in New York or elsewhere belong to the Continental service." The *Jersey* prisoners were understandably in no mood to listen to such technicalities. After failing, through addresses to Washington and to Congress, to get any promise of either exchange or relief, they addressed an open appeal to their countrymen, which appeared in the New York *Gazette* on June 17, 1782:

You may bid a final adieu to all your friends and relatives who are now on board the Jersey prison ships [*sic*] at New York, unless you rouse the government to comply with just and honorable proposals.... What is to be done? Are we to lie here and share the fate of our unhappy brothers who are dying daily? No, unless you relieve us immediately, we shall be under the necessity of leaving our country, in preservation of our lives.

The prisoners' threat to desert to the enemy was not wholly rhetoric. Although Dring said flatly, "During the whole period of my confinement, I never knew a single instance of enlistment from among the prisoners of the *Jersey*," Washington wrote in 1781 that, "conceiving themselves neglected, and seeing no prospect of relief, many of them entered into the enemy's service." Among the defectors was Ebenezer Fox. British recruiting officers made periodic visits to *Jersey*, and they caught Ebenezer at a suggestible moment. "We had just been trying to satisfy our hunger upon a piece of beef, which was so tough that no teeth could make an impression on it," he later explained, "when the officer descended between decks...." Ebenezer and eleven of his shipmates were very shortly marching under British escort—not guard—to lodgings on Long Island and thence to duty in His Majesty's service in the West Indies, from which they subsequently escaped.

There is little reason, however, to believe that enlistments in the British service were frequent among *Jersey* prisoners. When the war ended in 1783, the persuasive evidence to the contrary was a shipload of fourteen hundred gaunt prisoners to be released and the bones of eleven thousand spread across the sands of Remsen's beach. Twenty-five years later the *Jersey* survivors were writing ineradicable memoirs of their ordeal. The bleached bones of the dead were gathered for ceremonial burial by members of the Columbian Order, a patriotic society later to become somewhat less specialized as Tammany Hall. *Jersey* herself slowly rotted away at her Brooklyn anchorage, finally consumed by the sea.

Mr. Tourtellot's many books include William Diamond's Drum: The Beginning of the War of the American Revolution (*Doubleday, 1959*) *and* Lexington and Concord (*Norton, 1963*). *His principal sources for this article were memoirs written by* Jersey *ex-prisoners and published in the nineteenth century.*

Letters to the Editor

POLLUTING THE PRESTILE

Sir: Frank Graham has written a lively account of the controversy over the Prestile Stream ["That Mess on the Prestile," February, 1970]. Unfortunately, his journalistic effort on behalf of a worthy cause—environmental improvement—is marred by several inaccuracies.

First, the Prestile did not change from a pure trout stream to a polluted watercourse in 1960, when the Vahlsing potato-processing plant was built, or in 1965, when construction began on the Vahlsing sugar-beet refinery. Fish kills and blocked fish migrations were documented by state agencies as early as 1953. The fight over the discharges from the Vahlsing potato plant should be examined against the background of sewage discharges from Easton and Mars Hill, starch-factory discharges, and the dumping of potatoes along the stream. The B classification represented a goal, not a physical fact. The sugar-beet refinery has never polluted the Prestile. Reclassification was a temporary technical step, and it did not affect and has not affected the quality of the stream.

Second, the sugar-beet refinery did not take Vahlsing off the hook with respect to his potato-processing plant discharges. The temporary change in classification to D was in effect only from January, 1967, until October, 1967, when the stream was reclassified to C. The original change in classification from B to D, incidentally, was made at the insistence of bond counsel from the underwriters of the Maine Industrial Authority, not the federal government. The haste in the change was dictated by the necessity of having the refinery in operation in time to process the fall, 1966, crop of beets in order to retain the Maine sugar-beet allotment. . . .

Senator Muskie reluctantly supported the reclassification on three grounds: (a) the refinery could not be financed without it; (b) the reclassification would cover only the period of start-up for the plant and, in his view, should be restored to B at the end of that time; and (c) the

refinery would be designed and built with the most effective water utilization and waste treatment facilities. . . .

Third, the basic problem in dealing with the Prestile and similar difficulties on other Maine streams has been the antiquated Maine classification law, which requires legislative action for improvements in water quality standards and which does not provide adequate enforcement authority for the Environmental Improvement Commission. . . . In 1957 Governor Muskie initiated the first changes to upgrade the classification of Maine waters. . . .

I have cited the foregoing facts to counter the unfortunate impression . . . that Senator Muskie has been indifferent to pollution problems associated with industrial development in Maine and that he maintains a cozy relationship with Maine industrialists. William Caldwell, who is Mr. Graham's only authority for the Senator's "friendship" with Mr. Vahlsing, is not the most unbiased or accurate observer on the Maine political scene. Senator Muskie knew Mr. Vahlsing only slightly as a Maine businessman and not as a friend when Vahlsing entered the sugar-beet project, and he has dealt with Vahlsing as a constituent ever since. There has been no "friendship" to be "strained." . . .

> Donald E. Nicoll
> Administrative Assistant to
> Senator Edmund S. Muskie
> Washington, D.C.

Sir: Mr. Graham . . . has made two misstatements of fact . . . which create unfortunate innuendoes about my role as attorney general with respect to our efforts in the Maine courts to prevent Mr. Vahlsing from polluting the Prestile. . . . in May, 1968, nearly *two years* before Mr. Graham's article appeared, I initiated action against Potato Service, Inc., to enjoin that company from violating the terms of its waste discharge license. As a result of that action, Potato Service, Inc., has completely redesigned its waste treatment system, eliminating virtually all of the solids from its dis-

charge. In November, 1969 (*four months* before Mr. Graham's article appeared), a Maine superior court justice issued a decree establishing a timetable for complete cleanup by the company under court supervision. Potato Service, Inc., still has formidable problems with reducing the biochemical oxygen demand of its waste to the level permitted by its license, but under the terms of the decree it must plan, finance, and start construction of all necessary facilities to do so no later than October 1, 1973.

Mr. Graham . . . states that Maine "initiated but did not press a court action against Vahlsing." I do not know how Mr. Graham determines whether a suit has been "pressed.". . . After bringing the action, we secured a court order allowing our engineers access to the Vahlsing premises to inspect its facilities. We found that Vahlsing had redesigned his waste treatment facilities. No longer does he continually discharge mildly chlorinated potato waste into the Prestile. Instead, he has constructed a large lagoon (over ten acres in surface area) to hold the waste and pumps it from this lagoon through pipes to beet and potato fields where it is sprayed on the ground as fertilizer. We believe that our court action precipitated this maneuver. . . .

A part of the legal problem I have with Vahlsing, Inc., as Mr. Graham correctly points out, is that the legislature has by statute exempted that firm (as well as many other major polluters in Maine) from prosecution for violation of water-quality water classifications as long as a statutory cleanup timetable is met. The outer limit of this timetable is 1976. As a result, I was forced in the case of Vahlsing, Inc., to resort to my common-law powers as guardian of the public welfare and sue to have the firm declared a "public nuisance." As any lawyer will tell you, there are precious few standards for determining what a "public nuisance" is. . . .

> James S. Erwin
> Attorney General
> State of Maine
> Augusta, Maine

MR. GRAHAM REPLIES

Sir: . . . The point at issue in my article was Senator Muskie's decision to support the declassification of the Prestile. In the light of the state's claim that Vahlsing had violated antipollution regulations thirty-one times in the previous five years, this support cannot be justified. Trouble was inevitable.

It is true that the Prestile was polluted long before 1965. But the town of Mars Hill had invested in a treatment plant, and its efforts were undone by the potato wastes. Indeed, I wrote that by 1965 "The Prestile's quality was B only on the W.I.C.'s [Water Improvement Commission] books; in fact, it had become an open sewer."

I do not defend Maine's antiquated pollution laws. I simply said that the proposal to lower the Prestile's classification was a device to circumvent even those deficient laws.

I specifically said that the sugar-beet refinery "apparently has not become a source of pollution." I pointed out that by lowering the classification and by backing millions of dollars of loans to Vahlsing, state officials obviously had hindered the legal effort to secure abatement of the potato wastes. In this sense the state took the company "off the hook" and opened the way to the 1968 border incident.

Finally, I did not attempt to measure Senator Muskie's affection for Fred Vahlsing. Whatever its degree, however, I am certain it was strained by the fiasco on the New Brunswick border.

As for Mr. Erwin, I did not mention his name in the article, and I sympathize with his plight. In the passages he objected to I was making the point that neither he nor his predecessor could move effectively against the pollution without jeopardizing the state's investment in the sizable sugar-beet loans. The resultant flurry of legal activity which was slow to produce results became a source of the conservationists' dissatisfaction.

DELEHANTY'S FINEST

Sir: I read with great interest the article "The Policeman's Lot" in the February, 1970, issue. However, I do have one correction. On page 11 there is a picture of

Spring 3100

The Class of '23, Delehanty Institute

women doing exercises with the caption "Those above are members of the New York department's class of 1923" . . . [but] the picture you show is the graduating class of the Delehanty Institute Policewomen's Course in the year 1923. The man standing on the right-hand side of the picture, with the sweater on, is the late M. J. Delehanty, founder of the institute. . . .

> D. R. Howland
> Vice President
> The Delehanty Institute
> New York, New York

The information for our caption came from Spring 3100, *the official magazine of the New York City Police Department.—Ed.*

GROWING PAINS

Sir: . . . We have a fair city which one could say is beset by all the pollution and conservation problems rolled into one. . . .

When my husband and I, as newly-weds, arrived in Ventura (short for San Buenaventura) in 1948, it was a beautiful town of 18,000 built around two valuable commodities, agriculture and oil. Our geographical location was superb, between the ocean and the mountains. There was no influx or smog from the Los Angeles Basin. . . .

Now I will list our condition twenty-two years later—a mere twenty-two years later. . . .

1. Ventura has grown to 55,000. . . .
2. Valuable agricultural land, assessed beyond the point where it can be farmed, is disappearing at the rate of hundreds of acres per year.

3. The oil business has deteriorated locally (other than offshore, which brings no local tax money directly, only pollution) to the point where the county and city receive only a small fraction of what they used to get.

4. The heart of our city has become blocks and blocks of empty stores. . . .

5. Our grand old California Mission sits in a dreadfully depressed area of a once thriving downtown.

6. Our magnificent courthouse, built in 1912, which commands a splendid view on the side of a hill overlooking the ocean, has been allowed to deteriorate to the point where it is now being abandoned. . . .

7. Industry is being beckoned to the city to bring back a weakened tax base.

8. Trees, monuments, mountains, and sanity are all being plowed under or sheared off in the face of "progress."

9. Pollution is evident everywhere. . . .

Can we control our growth so it will not become a disaster? Can we stir up interest in preservation to the point where the taxpayer can see the advantage? . . . All growth and change are not necessarily progress. Ventura is the fastest growing county in the United States at this time, and the pain that goes with it is in the same ratio. . . .

> Barbara Udsen
> City Councilwoman
> San Buenaventura, California

WRECKERS' LOSSES

Sir: It is my pleasure to offer a correction to your article entitled "A Wrecker's Dozen" (February, 1970). The Emmanuel Shearith Israel Synagogue which you have pictured will not be torn down as part of an urban renewal project. The

Emmanuel Shearith Israel Synagogue

synagogue was placed on the National Register of Historic Places . . . before final go-ahead for federal funds was authorized. . . .

Robert Fink
Assistant to the Director
State Historical Society of Colorado
Denver, Colorado

Sir: . . . You will be pleased to know that the Destrehan Manor House is *not* doomed. The landmark is located on property owned by American Oil Company, where we once operated a refinery. After the refinery was abandoned and dismantled in 1959, the Manor House became the object of vandalism and other deterioration. This occurred despite our providing around-the-clock guard service after the refinery was closed.

We are now negotiating to sell the property. While doing so, we intend that the sale exclude the Manor House and some surrounding property. This we plan to donate to a local historical society with whom we've been working. We are hopeful that the land sale and donation will be completed within the near future. . . .

Harry A. Swanson
Manager, Field Service
American Oil Company
Chicago, Illinois

A PLEA FOR RESTRAINT

Sir: . . . At various times in the past twenty-five years I have joined and supported organizations devoted to "conservation." I have found, to my sorrow, that most of the people (and organizations) have exceedingly narrow interests and little interest or understanding of conservation. Therefore, although we must pursue conservation and preservation with increased vigor, it is imperative that we also devote considerable effort toward teaching our people what conservation is . . .

Above all, we have to inspire great numbers of people to "put their money where their mouth is." . . . It has been my observation that hunters are the only single group who have been willing to spend considerable sums of money in support of conservation per se. All others lobby for the "government" to spend *its* money for their pet projects. Too many individuals and organizations

spend far too much effort fighting other conservation and preservation activities and far too little . . . on actual projects of lasting value. . . .

I am not a hunter, fisherman, camper, or bird-watcher and have no personal interest in a "wilderness" area or the like.

Since we ran "A Memorandum to Oliver Wendell Holmes" in our February, 1970, issue, a number of readers interested in helping to preserve the U.S.S. *Constitution* have written us, and some have sent donations for us to forward. "Project Old Ironsides" no longer exists, and the Navy says that the ship is being provided regular maintenance inspections and that there is no lack of funds for continuing her upkeep.

According to Rear Admiral J. C. Wylie, Commandant, First Naval District, Boston, "Ever since the rebuilding of the *Constitution* in the 1920's, the Congress has appropriated all the money needed for preservation of the ship; over the past five years this has averaged close to a quarter of a million dollars a year. In the autumn of 1969, for instance, as soon as the summer tourist rush subsided, work was begun replacing the entire after end of the spar deck and replacing the strength members in the stern of the ship. This work was completed before the 1970 summer tourist season. The ship is scheduled to be drydocked, as she is about every seven years, in 1972."

Such contributions as we have received have been forwarded to Admiral Wylie for the possible purchase and maintenance of artifacts and memorabilia associated with the *Constitution*. These moneys have gone into a museum fund especially established for this purpose. Those who wish to donate to the fund should address their contributions to the U.S.S. *Constitution* Museum Fund, First Naval District Headquarters, 495 Summer Street, Boston, Massachusetts 02210.

I am concerned that there is a threat to the ecological balance which allows man to live. Once that balance is destroyed, we will not have an opportunity to recover. Until the exact point of danger is determined, it will be exceedingly wise to exercise restraint . . .

Jesse D. Thompson
Clarksville, Arkansas

JUVENES DUM SUMUS

Dear Establishment Freaks: Please take my name off of your mailing list. I am not interested in your books or your "American Heritage." I'm afraid I belong to that group on the other side that grew up in the 60's. I have heard all I want to about the neat 20's and 30's from my parents. I have borne personal witness to the culmination of that keen heritage. Uptight White amerika is on the run and my generation intends to keep it running. Amerika had a good thing going until Alexander Hamilton opened his big mouth and the revolution was sold out to the conservatives. We just might have to take a second shot at pulling off another revolution by 1976. I learned all about my Heritage in school, sap that I was I believed it. So send your books to all the little old John Birch ladies. I'm busy trying to clean up just one of the messes you dudes have tried to cover up, the native people of this country that managed to survive the genocide.

Thanks for the free envelope.

Don Petterson
Culbertson, Montana

This is spelt as received. The German form of the word America, *in the polite lexicon of youth, signifies their astonishing belief that we have gone Nazi.—Ed.*

Sir: Because my family already receives AMERICAN HERITAGE I think it would be unwise to add another membership subscription, but I could not let this opportunity go by without letting you know how much I enjoy it.

Your magazine gives a very good look into the very human history of our country. By showing the diversity of our nation's history you combat the current oversimplification of America's past. . . .

James J. Moynihan, Jr.
Fairfield University
Fairfield, Connecticut

A Letter
from the Arctic

The letter excerpted below seems an eloquent way to introduce the article on the following pages by Walter Sullivan, science editor of the New York Times. *The writer of the letter, Samuel Wright, is a professor of social ecology who resigned his post to live with his wife in an isolated 12-by-12-foot log cabin in Alaska's Brooks Range, north of the Arctic Circle. There they are writing and filming the story of "this last great wilderness." "A Letter from the Arctic," relayed by bush pilot, first appeared in* The Living Wilderness, *the quarterly publication of The Wilderness Society. It is with the society's and Mr. Wright's kind permission that we present it here.*

As I write this, a great caravan of heavily laden trucks is growling over a new winter road which yesterday reached the Eskimo village in Anaktuvuk Pass at the central top of the range. Yesterday wrote the end of Anaktuvuk Pass as it was, a small village of inland Eskimos still dependent upon migrating herds of caribou. It may have written the beginning of the end of the great caribou herds, majestic mountain sheep, and the wolf. It was certainly the end of thousands of years of solitude, as the great diesel trucks thundered up the John River valley on their way to the North Slope and the great oil strike near Prudhoe Bay on the Arctic Ocean.

For many millenniums this great range of mountains north of the Yukon in Alaska not only sheltered caribou herds and bands of mountain sheep but provided breeding grounds for myriad birds. Athabascan Indians and inland Eskimos shared this great wilderness, living out their lives as an integral part of a balanced ecology. To the Indian and caribou-hunting Eskimo, this was more than home. It was ten thousand years of Eden, where the bear and wolf gave their pelts, and the fish flashing in lakes and streams after break-up were fat and abundant.

This is the way it was in what is now called the Brooks Range, that great escarpment which stretches over five hundred miles from Canada to the western coast north of the Arctic Circle in Alaska. Because of its inaccessibility and because the winters are long and cold, this last great wilderness on the American continent is still relatively pristine, a resource from which man can yet gain sustenance for his spirit, know his roots, and perhaps save his soul. . . .

Who speaks for wilderness? Nearly everyone says it is a value we must not lose and expresses regret at what seems to be the inevitable ambition of civilization to bring every niche on earth under domestication. But when a choice for wilderness or domestication is to be made, progress, money, exploitation, if not encouraged, are condoned. With the North Slope oil strike already producing millionaires, and an estimate of enough reserves to make the United States virtually independent of foreign sources, few question that the fields will be brought into full production. But need we destroy a wilderness in the process? . . .

America's greed for oil has drastically upset the ecological
balance of Alaska's North Slope, and the end is not in sight

OUR LAST
GREAT WILDERNESS

By WALTER SULLIVAN

Even when the sun is out, Point Barrow on the Arctic Ocean, northernmost point of Alaska, looks uninviting, although life abounds there.

On August 16, 1826, after long weeks of frustrating and perilous travel along the north coast of Alaska, the British explorer Sir John Franklin decided to abandon his bold ambition—completing the exploration of the North American coastline. The cluster of gravel banks where a conspiracy of storm, fog, drifting ice, and approaching winter forced him to turn back—still shown on maps as the Return Islands—lay off an indentation that he named Prudhoe Bay.

Less than a century and a half later this remote spot has become an arena for fierce, almost frantic competition among the world's largest oil empires, and a focus of conservationist outrage. The gravel bars and shallow waters that made life miserable for Franklin's men, with their small boats, have confounded those operating the largest ships ever built—the oil magnates seeking to extract the newly discovered oil beneath Prudhoe Bay.

The mission assigned to Franklin was to follow the uncharted coast from the mouth of the Mackenzie River in Canada across the top of Alaska to Bering Strait. Once Sir John's party had passed from British to what was then Russian territory, travelling in boats that could be hauled over the sea ice when necessary, the mountains paralleling the coast had receded to the south, leaving a broad plain of marshy tundra between the shore and foothills.

At the same time the weather had become very foggy, perhaps, Sir John thought, because of the sodden nature of the coastal plain. For a week he had been unable to take any astronomical sights to learn his position, and for days the party was confined to a gravelly spit that they named Foggy Island.

The fog curtailed the caribou hunting on which they depended for fresh food, and there was only limited driftwood for their fires. When they tried to continue westward, they soon bogged down again, this time on one of the gravel banks they were to christen the Return Islands.

The bemedalled Englishman below, Sir John Franklin, reached Prudhoe Bay, off Alaska's North Slope, in 1826. He was forced to turn back because of fog, ice, and worsening weather. Franklin and his party died on a later voyage while searching for a northwest passage across the top of the continent. More than forty rescue parties, including the ships Alert *and* Discovery *above, were sent in search of his expedition, thereby gaining invaluable information about the frigid wastes. The centuries-long quest for a passageway through the ice-clogged Arctic Ocean culminated last summer in the voyage of the oil tanker* Manhattan, *pictured at right.*

After two days the sky cleared just long enough for observations to determine their position. The signs were all ominous. The season was late, and the fact that no Eskimos had been seen suggested that the region was inhospitable even to that hardy and resourceful people. Hence, on August 18, when the weather seemed at least tolerable, they began their return:

As the waves were still very high to seaward [Sir John wrote], we attempted to proceed inside of the reefs, but as the boats were constantly taking the ground, we availed ourselves of the first channel that was sufficiently deep to pull on outside of them. The swell being too great there for the use of oars, the sails were set double reefed, and the boats beat to eastward against the wind, between the drift ice and the shallow water.

Thus ended the first visit of modern man to Prudhoe Bay. Sir John returned to the Arctic in 1845 to attempt a passage from the Atlantic to the Pacific across the top of North America—the long-sought Northwest Passage. His ships were caught in the ice, and ultimately all 129 men of the expedition perished; but the expeditions sent to search for them—more than forty parties in all—added enormously to knowledge of the region and thus helped to make possible the historic trip of the giant tanker *Manhattan* in 1969.

Sir John and his men saw the land they discovered from the grimmest possible perspective, as do, to some extent, those laboring there now to find oil—fog, unpredictable ice floes, biting winds, frustrating gravel banks, a largely featureless shore, and an almost impassable swamp if one seeks, randomly, to walk inland.

The magnificent belt of mountains that parallels the coast is too far south to be usually visible. Yet those mountains, which span the entire width of northern Alaska from Canada to near the Bering Strait, together with the slope between them and the Arctic Ocean constitute the largest and least spoiled wilderness remaining within the United States. While the mountains have various local names, the system as a whole is known as the Brooks Range. It is, in fact, the northernmost extremity of the Rocky Mountain system. The foothills and the apron of tundra between them and the sea are known as the North Slope.

Near the coast the North Slope is not a slope at all, except to an imperceptible degree. It is like the sea—a great, monotonous, flat expanse that, to those who love it, has a grandeur without counterpart. One's vision is opened to limitless horizons. One sees the march of clouds above and the march of seasons below in a way denied those hemmed in by walls or forests.

One of the most striking features of this region as seen from the air is the patterning of the surface much like that of an alligator skin. The extreme cold shrinks the ground until a polygonal series of cracks is formed. The cracks eventually fill with water, which freezes, leaving a system of tundra polygons enclosed by veins of ice.

To walk the tundra in summer is a chore, but well worth the effort. The dry winds blowing in from the ice-covered ocean bring little precipitation, but what there is stays on the surface, because the ground below is frozen; and since the region is flat, little flows away. The result is an endless series of puddles large and small.

These ponds are the summer home of all kinds of waterfowl, including phalaropes, whose heads jerk back and forth as they swim like little toy ducks. A remarkable feature of the tens of thousands of lakes south of Point Barrow, northernmost tip of United States territory, is that virtually all of them are elongated in precisely the same direction—slightly west of north. The orientation of the lakes has nothing to do with local geology, and they were not gouged by a flowing ice sheet. Scientists working on the North Slope are still seeking an explanation.

Walk across the tundra with your eyes alert and you will see the signs of an extraordinary ecology. Snaking through the covering of grass, sedge, lichens, and moss that is often knee-deep are countless little channels that hug the ground. Every now and then mouselike creatures scurry along one of these passages.

They are lemmings. Their channels are formed as tunnels under the snow during the winter, for lemmings do not hibernate and must push under the snow

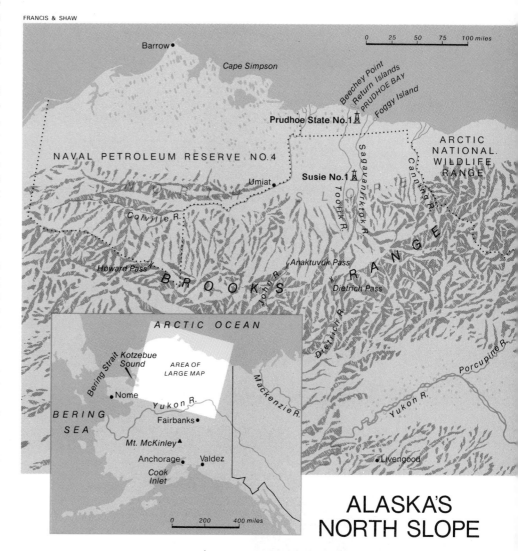

FRANCIS & SHAW

ALASKA'S NORTH SLOPE

in search of cotton grass and other food. At the peak of the lemming population cycle that comes every three or four years, the tundra is swarming with the animals. Overhead a jaeger, a predatory gull with a spearlike tail, may be circling, waiting his chance to swoop on one of them. Here and there on the ground lie objects that look like black golf balls. These are owl pellets—the regurgitated remains of lemmings eaten by snowy owls, which digest the nourishing parts of the animal, then regurgitate a snug ball of fur and bones.

What fascinates the ecologists is the relative simplicity of relationships between the various life forms that make the North Slope beautiful and exciting. To a certain extent the larger animals all wax and wane in step with the lemming cycle. When the lemmings are plentiful, with as many as two hundred per acre, those who prey on them thrive: the jaegers, owls, and foxes in particular, but also, to some extent, the wolves, weasels, and wolverines.

The great puzzle is what causes the lemming cycles. What, too, accounts for tales of their mass suicides, when thousands plunge into the sea? Early explanations included such farfetched ideas as their desire to reach an ancestral home,

a lost continent west of Norway, where mass lemming plunges are famous.

A more recent thesis has been that because of their extraordinary rate of multiplication they overwhelm their food supply. (The female gestates her young in twenty days and bears as many as thirteen in a litter. The newly born are ready to breed within three weeks.) According to this theory the forage, depleted by overgrazing, takes two or three years to recover in the harsh climate, and so lemming hordes set out in search of new pastures, plunging into every body of water that stands in their way, be it a narrow pond or the ocean.

It has recently been reported, however, that the population "crashes" occur *before* the food is exhausted, and the dying animals are not skinny. Some believe a change in blood chemistry, caused either by the stress of overcrowding or by a long spell of warm weather, affects the lemming brain, leading to erratic behavior and finally death.

Despite such puzzles, the ecology of the North Slope is far simpler than that of warmer environments, where many more life forms and other factors interact. Hence the North Slope is uniquely suited for the study of ecology.

Not that it lacks diversity. At Barrow

there are about one hundred species of hollow-stemmed, or vascular, plants. During the two-month growing season the tundra abounds in color—purple and white anemones, poppies, saxifrage, and roses. Because the time for seeds to germinate and establish themselves is short, the tundra plants tend to belong to species that propagate themselves by spreading, like strawberry shoots or ivy, rather than by seed.

However, the continuous daylight of early summer helps make up for the shortness of the season. At Prudhoe Bay the sun does not set from May 14 to July 30 (and it does not rise from November 24 to January 17).

In winter the sharp demarkation between North Slope and Arctic Ocean tends to disappear. Both are frozen and snow-covered. Walking out to sea from the Prudhoe Bay shore this spring I found it impossible to tell when you left land and were walking on the sea. Farther out, though, the pack ice is forever in motion. Borne by wind and current, the floes grind and shriek against one another, sometimes overriding when an onshore wind presses them against the coast, sometimes buckling to form giant pressure ridges.

Polar bears roam the ice floes; grizzlies

are numerous in the Brooks Range foothills. In the mountains one may see wolves following a band of migrating caribou or, if one is lucky, a loping wolverine who pauses every few dozen yards to rise on his hind feet and look around, like an oversized raccoon. He is said to be so ferocious that, although smaller than a wolf, he will drive a whole pack from their kill.

While the sweep of the tundra and the treeless foothills is magnificent, the jagged peaks of the Brooks Range are breathtaking. The mystery, beauty, and isolation of those mountains have enslaved the souls of many visitors, including myself.

Probably the first white man to cross the Brooks Range was Ensign (later Rear Admiral) W. L. Howard, who had been with a Navy expedition exploring tributaries of the Yukon in 1886. He penetrated the mountains and met a band of friendly Eskimos, who led him across what is now Howard Pass to the North Slope. There he descended to the Colville River, which he found to be an Eskimo trade route.

There were two distinct Eskimo cultures: the Nunamiut Eskimos, who lived a nomadic, inland life heavily dependent on caribou hunting; and the coastal Tariamiut Eskimos, whose base of operations was usually a village centered on a "dance house" and led by a whaling chief. Survival of the two groups depended heavily on trade between them.

Howard remained with the inland Eskimos until, with the arrival of spring, the ice broke thunderously from the rivers and the trading parties began to head downstream for the coast. Howard found these Eskimos gay and helpful travelling companions, and he became the first white man to reach the Arctic Ocean from the Alaskan interior.

In 1901 and 1924 the mountains were crossed via other routes. Then, in the thirties, a young man named Robert Marshall felt the call of the Brooks Range and devoted several years to its exploration. Marshall was a New Yorker of independent means with a doctor's degree in botany from the Johns Hopkins University.

So deeply moved was Marshall by the beauty and solitude of the Brooks Range and other such virgin regions that he became instrumental in the establishment of the national wilderness areas that now preserve select tracts from harmful intrusion. This he was able to accomplish in the late 1930's as chief of the Division of Recreation and Lands in the United States Forest Service. One of the preserves, in Montana, now bears his name: the Bob Marshall Wilderness Area.

Marshall's successive penetrations of the Brooks Range, during which he followed stream beds and ascended mountains to take bearings for his map making, showed the region to be unique. The mountains, none more than ten thousand feet high, are not as lofty as those of the central Rockies, but the harsh polar environment has carved them into pinnacles, canyons, and jumbled ridges nothing less than awesome.

Marshall told, as none had before, of the wonders of this region. At one point he came upon a lake more than a mile long, hemmed in by towering slopes that vanished into the clouds. Waterfalls dropped from the cloud-shrouded heights into the lake and its tributary streams.

"Nothing I had ever seen, Yosemite or the Grand Canyon or Mount McKinley rising from the Susitna, had given me such a sense of immensity," Marshall wrote afterward of this spot. Yet he limited the circulation of his books on the Brooks Range, apparently fearful that his glowing descriptions might generate a deluge of tourists. These mountains,

Above, the almost flat tundra touching the Arctic Ocean is highly vulnerable to erosion when its plant cover is destroyed. In stark contrast is the snow-clad Brooks Range on the North Slope's southern border. Like those at the left, its peaks average between a mile and two miles in height.

he felt, should forever be preserved for those willing to endure hardship to find solitude.

There is something glorious in traveling beyond the ends of the earth [he wrote], in living in a different world which men have not discovered, in cutting loose from the bonds of world-wide civilization. Such life holds a joy and an exhilaration which most explorers today cannot understand, with their radios and aeroplanes which make the remotest corners of the world just a few days or even hours away in distance. Modern mechanical ingenuity has brought many good things to the world, but in the long list of high values which it has ruined, one of the greatest is the value of isolation.

Marshall could hardly have guessed how soon the modern world would invade this last great wilderness. When Ensign Howard crossed the mountains in 1886, he found that some of the natives were stoking their fires with oil-soaked shale. In 1906 Ernest de Koven Leffingwell of the United States Geological Survey, who explored the coastal area near Prudhoe Bay, found oil seeping out of the ground. And there were Eskimo tales of an entire lake of oil near Cape Simpson, west of Prudhoe Bay. In 1917 Alexander Malcolm Smith, better known as Sandy Smith, found the "lake," fed by a large seepage, and within four years oil companies had begun staking claims in the area.

 *Alaska thaw: a roller-coaster effect is unintentionally achieved by railroad tracks as the frozen ground melts unevenly beneath.*

The Navy in those days was concerned with having access to sufficient fuel reserves for its fleet, newly converted from coal to oil. Three oil fields in the United States proper had been set aside as Naval Petroleum Reserves, including one at Teapot Dome in Wyoming.

In 1923 Secretary of the Interior Albert B. Fall acted to set aside the entire western part of the North Slope as Naval Petroleum Reserve Number 4. Hardly had he done so when it was discovered that he had accepted $100,000 or more to allow a private oil company to ex-

ploit the Teapot Dome reserve. He was fined $100,000 and imprisoned.

Meanwhile, the Navy asked the Geological Survey to make a study of Naval Petroleum Reserve Number 4, better known as Pet 4. This was completed in 1926, but no further action was taken until the enormously increased fuel consumption of World War II caused alarm. Reconnaissance in 1943 and 1944 disclosed seeps near Umiat, and an assessment suggested that an oil-bearing area "of indicated major importance" lay within the reserve.

Using amphibious techniques perfected during the war, the Navy landed equipment on the Arctic coast and hauled it across the tundra to various drilling sites, primarily at Umiat and near the coast at Cape Simpson (both areas of extensive seepage). Airstrips and base camps were built. When the war ended the work went on, and by 1953 a total of thirty-six test wells and forty-four smaller core holes had been drilled, some of them twelve thousand feet deep. At times as many as five hundred men worked on the North Slope, and a total of $47,000,000 was spent.

The results were disappointing. Oil-bearing structures were penetrated, the largest reservoir being that at Umiat with an estimated seventy million barrels, but this was by no means enough to justify the enormous cost of Arctic

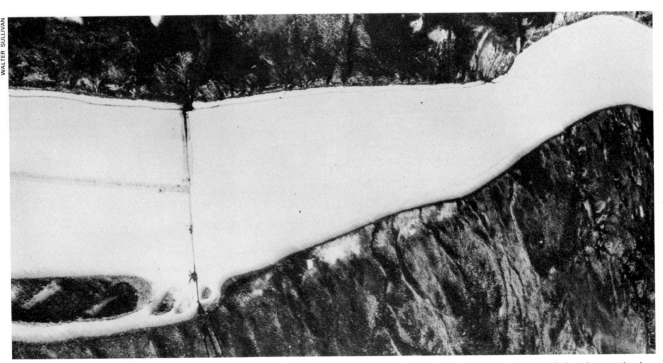

In winter the frozen Yukon River serves as underpinning for transporting supplies. The vertical line near the center of the photograph above is a log bridge; an airstrip has been cleared from the ice to the left. The truck on the opposite page is heading across the melting tundra.

As whites moved in along the coast areas, many Eskimo villages turned into slums.

petroleum extraction and transport.

In 1946 one party went east of Pet 4 to explore along the Sagavanirktok River —now known to oilmen all over the world as the Sag River. In that area, alongside Prudhoe Bay, geologists reported some promising "closed anticlines"—domed structures produced millions of years ago by folding of rock layers, within which oil tends to accumulate. However, no drilling was done.

Thus, sad to relate, prospectors for the Navy missed making the great strike. Had they done so, the history of the North Slope might have been quite different, for the Navy would have been far more inclined to hold the reservoirs of oil in reserve than would commercial firms answerable to profit-hungry stock-

holders looking for big dividends.

The final report to the Navy, when Pet 4 prospecting was halted in 1953, said that "the likelihood of usable petroleum deposits in the area are poor." However, it noted, usable gas accumulations had been tapped. One well, near Barrow, was supplying that community with gas, obviating the need for an expensive delivery of fuel via the Arctic Ocean.

While the Navy-sponsored exploration did not hit the jackpot, it did demonstrate the extreme vulnerability of the North Slope to disturbance by man. When giant tractors hauled sled trains of heavy equipment across the snow-covered tundra, little or no harm was done. But if this occurred after melting had exposed the vegetation and the covering layer was destroyed, the otherwise permanently frozen muck below, known as permafrost, melted in the summer sun. The "road" became a muddy canal. If there was any slope, this soon became a torrent.

As noted by Dr. Max Brewer, head of the Naval Arctic Research Laboratory at Barrow, during a 1969 ecology conference, twelve feet of surface material could be eroded in this manner within two summers. Drilling has shown that the ground beneath the tundra south of Barrow is frozen to a depth of 1,330 feet.

The Army also had its troubles with permafrost. During World War II it was called upon to build airfields, hangars, and roads in the Alaskan interior and discovered how little it knew about the peculiarities of such terrain. When an airstrip of pierced planking or pavement was laid over a shallow layer of fill, the summer sun, shining on the surface day and night, generated enough heat to melt the frozen ground underneath. The result was that some parts of the runways sank and others did not, producing a graceful roller-coaster effect. When buildings were set directly on permafrost, they too settled in a lopsided manner, at times breaking apart.

From experience (and from studying Russian publications on the subject) the Army engineers learned to lay a bed of gravel about five feet thick over the permafrost as insulation before building anything on top of it. An alternate scheme was to drive pilings down into the frozen

ground and then set the structure on top of the pilings, well clear of contact with the ground.

The wartime activities of the Army and Navy also demonstrated how easily the treeless landscape of the North Slope is defaced. In the Pacific Islands the war scars were soon overgrown, but in the open vastness of the tundra a single oil drum, abandoned vehicle, or crumbling Quonset hut can be seen for miles. Indeed, the oil drums used to fuel the tracked behemoths that hauled equipment across the tundra are the most common manifestations of civilization in that land. As one colonel in the Army Engineers wryly remarked, "The fifty-gallon oil drum is the new state flower of Alaska."

It was not only the hunt for oil that strewed steel drums across much of the Arctic. In the early postwar years fear of Soviet attack led to the construction of a chain of radar stations from Bering Strait to Greenland—the Distant Early Warning net, or DEW-line.

It was an effort that projected many Eskimos from the Stone Age to the age of electronics. As with the drill rigs, much of the heavy equipment was moved in winter when giant sleds could be hauled across the frozen tundra. Working conditions were frightful, with sub-zero winds blowing unchecked off the Arctic Ocean.

Eskimos were ideal for such work— hardy, resourceful. The best of the Eskimo "cat-skinners" who drove the giant "cats," or tractors, learned to make repairs far from home base even in a cruel blizzard. Some, paid generous overtime wages on the same basis as men imported from warmer climes, were said to be making ten thousand dollars a year. With no sensible way to spend their money, they leafed through mail-order catalogues and, I was told, had such items as wide-screen television sets airfreighted to Barrow, even though their unpainted shacks had no electric power and there was no local television reception anyway.

However, such prosperity was exceptional. As will be seen, the Eskimo population as a whole was slipping into poverty and a crisis of adjustment.

The hunt for Alaskan oil began again shortly after Alaska achieved statehood in 1958. In 1964 the state applied to the

An Eskimo woman stands beside her makeshift tent on Kotzebue Sound, in northwestern Alaska. The men in the family are away on a walrus hunt.

federal Bureau of Land Management for control over some two million acres along the coast of the North Slope between Pet 4 on the west (bounded by the Colville River) and the Arctic National Wildlife Range to the east (bounded by the Canning River). The Wildlife Range, embracing 8,900,000 acres and the most scenic part of the Brooks Range, is open to only limited access, although it could someday be invaded by drilling crews if the government so authorized.

The federal government opened up some of the land that it retained, south of the state's newly acquired land, and the state subdivided its sector into a checkerboard of 2,560-acre tracts. Some 900,000 acres of this land were auctioned off in lease sales from 1964 to 1967, for which the state received $12,000,000 in "bonus bids." These gave the purchaser

the right to drill. If he struck oil, he would have to pay additional fees in royalties and taxes.

After a quick look at the geology of the area, Richfield (later Atlantic-Richfield) and Humble decided to gobble up a tenth of these leases and also to gamble on a costly effort to drill into a suspected anticline on federal land sixty miles south of Prudhoe Bay, between the Sag and Toolik rivers.

During the summer of 1965 and the following winter, a prodigious effort—involving what was reportedly the most ambitious nonmilitary airlift in Alaskan history—moved about four million pounds of pipe, rigging, fuel, bulldozers, house trailers, and trucks, plus a drill especially designed for use in a frigid climate, to the chosen site, christened Susie No. 1. By October, 1966, the drill

had penetrated to 13,500 feet without striking oil. The bill for this "dry well" was $4,500,000.

However, the analysis of subsurface structures had revealed two promising anticlines, or humps, in buried strata near the coast, one near the Colville River and one at Prudhoe Bay. Each was about twenty square miles in area.

In the winter of 1967 the rig at Susie No. 1 was transported to Prudhoe Bay across the frozen tundra in fifty cat-train trips. On each trip three giant tractors hauled sleds carrying forty tons of cargo. On April 8, 1967, drilling began on what was to be the historic Prudhoe State No. 1 well (so called because it was leased from the state). Hardly a month had passed before the spring thaw weakened ice on the lake where supply planes were landing, and operations then had to be suspended for a long time.

Drilling began again in November, and a few weeks later there were indications that the drill was chewing its way through black shale or mudstone. If there was oil lower down, it could be trapped under such an impermeable layer.

At the start of 1968 came the first hint. Gas was detectable in the mud used for drilling. On January 16 Atlantic-Richfield, which was doing the drilling on behalf of itself and Humble, reported a "substantial flow of gas" from a depth of 8,500 feet.

Then, on a bitter February day, Jim Keasler, a drill engineer, decided to run a gas-flow test. The temperature was 40° below zero with a strong wind blowing as he rigged a flow line to carry any emerging gas far away from the wellhead.

At 2:13 P.M., when he began to clear the drill pipe and allow gas to come to the surface, it was already dark. An hour later there was a roar and burst of fire as a jet of gas blew out of the flow line, sending flames fifty feet into the air.

For an hour or more the flickering plume of fire lighted the snows of the North Slope, and a few days later oil had begun flowing from the well like water.

The flow from a thick sandstone layer 8,656 feet below the surface eventually rose to 2,415 barrels a day. Microscopic fossils from this layer showed that it had been laid down during the Triassic period, some two hundred million years ago.

Was this strike a fluke? Or had a major oil field been tapped? The oilmen were eager to find out by drilling a "confirmation" well on the Sag River, seven miles southeast of Prudhoe State No. 1.

Atlantic-Richfield and Humble contracted for use of an unused rig on the Colville. They hauled it down the frozen river to the Arctic Ocean and then over the sea ice between the offshore islands and the coast to Prudhoe Bay and the Sag River site.

When the drilling began it was spring, which normally would have brought operations to a halt, but in their eagerness the oilmen decided, for the first time, to drill through the summer. By dint of

ingenious and expensive measures, such as covering the drill site and an airstrip with a five-foot layer of gravel to prevent thawing of the permafrost foundation, this was accomplished.

Throughout the summer the rig, Sag River State No. 1, drilled ever deeper. Within five months it had struck a three-hundred-foot layer of sand in the same Triassic formation as that tapped by the Prudhoe well, and a test drew 2,300 barrels a day from the bottom fifteen feet of this layer.

The two oil companies then asked the prestigious and reputedly conservative oil consulting firm of DeGolyer and MacNaughton, in Dallas, to assess the field. Their reply: "In our opinion, this important discovery could develop into a field with recoverable reserves of some five to ten billion barrels of oil, which would rate it as one of the largest petroleum accumulations known to the world today."

When news of the great strike came out, the ambitions of every man in the oil business caught fire. The most urgent problem for all was to decide which of the remaining blocks of unleased land was likely to be a fortune-maker. To this end as much information as possible had to be obtained by drilling on blocks already leased.

The result was a series of frantic battles with distance, cold, and other Arctic impediments. A combine of Mobil and Phillips Petroleum moved a rig by barge to the Prudhoe Bay area via Great Slave Lake and the Mackenzie River; British Petroleum also used barges, but made its approach from the west, through the Aleutians and the Bering Sea.

Meanwhile Walter J. Hickel, Alaska's governor, soon to be named Secretary of the Interior, had decided to give the trucking companies a hand by building a "winter road" from the terminus of the Alaskan highway system at Livengood, 470 miles through the Brooks Range to Prudhoe Bay. The road would be usable only when the ground was frozen, and it was a race against time to finish it before the spring thaw.

Tractor trains, hauling giant sleds, had already made the trip in winter. One of them, with 380 tons of pipe for the Pan American Petroleum Corporation plus enough fuel to drive its trac-

RALPH CRANE. *Life* MAGAZINE © TIME. INC.

The boiler and steam system above provides heat and electricity for a company camp. Next to oil rigs such as the one on the opposite page, the power plant is the most important machinery in a drilling operation. Work crews at some sites have indiscriminately dumped discarded gear across the tundra.

Snowy owl

Lemming

Saxifrage

Bistort

*Hanging in the balance of the North Slope's future is a wide variety
of animals and plants that have adapted to the severe environment
after thousands of years of evolution. Caribou—such as those at right
crossing a river bar—may find their ancient migration routes blocked
by man-made structures; unless buried underground or built high on
stilts, a pipeline, for example, could seriously impede the movement
of the herds between their summer and winter pastures. The little
lemming, top left, is a key to many life cycles; when he thrives, those
who prey on him, such as the snowy owl and the wolverine, thrive
too. Biologists fear that certain species could be wiped out in a decade.*

Grizzly bear

Polar bear

Wolverine

Timber wolf

tors the entire route (there are no filling stations in the North), was creeping toward a well site sixty miles southwest of Prudhoe Bay (Kavık No. 1, not many miles ahead of the twenty-two-man road-building crew.

To carry the road across the Yukon at Stevens Village, the local Athabascan Indians were recruited. They laid logs, woven with metal cable, across the river ice and then pumped water from the river to cover the logs with ice. The construction crew reached this 1,500-foot bridge at the start of 1969 but were halted by a spell of extremely cold weather. Finally, on January 14, the temperature climbed to a "mild" 49° below zero, and they set forth in the almost continuous darkness with headlights helping the bulldozers as they gouged and slashed their way through the scrub forest.

The route followed the John River, where Bob Marshall had wondered at the grandeur of the Brooks Range, to Anaktuvuk Pass, where there was one of the last inland settlements of Nunamiut Eskimos. Archaeological remains in the pass show that their ancestors have lived there for thousands of years, deriving food, clothing, and even their skin-covered huts from caribou herds channelled through the pass. The pass is also a convergence of flyways that carry migratory birds to the North Slope from as far away as Asia and South America.

Now, however, the rock walls of the pass thundered to the sound of diesel engines, and the construction crew contracted with the Eskimos to mark the final 182 miles of the road across the windswept tundra to Prudhoe Bay. This the Eskimos did by tying bundles of brush and topping each bundle with a red flag.

On March 12 the road was finished, and in the few weeks before the spring thaw, some 340 tractor-trailer loads fought their way north. Hardly a month after its completion I flew along the road and through the pass. The spring sun had done its work. The road was a long black scar across the landscape. Before the summer was out, much of it was a muddy canal. In the words of one oil company executive it had proven to be "somewhat less than satisfactory."

The road, called the Walter J. Hickel Ice Highway, became a focal point of in-dignation to those who feared an ecological disaster. They argued that it had set in motion an irreversible process in which melting would steadily widen the scar, making a muddy barrier to caribou herds, whose survival depends on migration between summer and winter pastures. (Caribou are still plentiful in northern Alaska. The Porcupine River herd in the east is now estimated at 140,-000 and the western herd at 300,000.) It was also argued that muddy water running down the roadbed was polluting streams, interfering with the spawning of salmon and other fish.

Secretary Hickel sought to shrug off the episode. "So they've scarred the tundra," he told Science magazine. "That's one road, twelve feet wide, in an area as big as the state of California." Nevertheless, although last winter the ice road was reopened, as well as a spur along the projected pipeline route into Dietrich Pass, Mr. Hickel seems to be moving cautiously on the pipeline itself.

Meanwhile the race to prepare for the lease bidding gained momentum. New airstrips sprang up like dandelions on a spring lawn. By late summer there were seven within seventy miles of Prudhoe Bay; at the airport in Fairbanks one could see as many as ten of the giant Hercules planes lined up for loading. Drilling equipment was stacked alongside the taxiways. The tundra, a few years ago the loneliest place in the world, had lights twinkling across its vastness in the busy winter of 1968–69 as drill crews raced to reach the oil-bearing layers. By the time, in September, 1969, when a representative of the state of Alaska stepped to a microphone in Anchorage and called on seven hundred oilmen to cease their excited murmuring, thirty-seven wells had been drilled on the Slope, and twenty-four seismic crews had roamed the tundra, setting off explosions and making measurements.

"It is 8:13 A.M. on the tenth day of September, 1969," said the man at the microphone. "My name is Tom Kelly...."

Thus began one of the most dramatic scenes in Alaskan history. The state had called for sealed bids on the available North Slope tracts. Each of the envelopes contained not only a bid but a check for 20 per cent of the proffered amount. At the airport a jet stood ready to rush the checks to New York for immediate deposit, lest even one day's interest be lost.

The preparation for this meeting also had its dramatic elements. The executives of ten oil companies chartered a train for five days and had it run continuously back and forth through the scenic country between Calgary and Edmonton, Alberta, while they worked out details of their joint bids. No one was allowed to leave the train.

The state of Alaska had also been busy, preparing "floor bids" on each tract. These, in effect, were assessments on the basis of which the state could refuse a bid if it seemed too low. As customary, those companies exploring the North Slope had been required to submit all their data, including drilling logs, to the state to help in preparation of these floor bids. There was an obvious danger that rival companies might gain access to this information, and the records were daily carried to and from a vault under guard.

The audience in the Anchorage auditorium watched intently as the first of 1,105 sealed bids on the 179 tracts up for sale was opened. The bidding began strong. A combination of Gulf, British Petroleum, and BP Alaska offered $96,-000,000 for six tracts. In the end, after a few bids had been rejected as too low, 164 tracts had been leased for bonus bids totalling a little over $900,000,000.

There had never been anything like it in the history of the oil business. And this for the right to drill on a relatively small area of ground in a vast territory bought from Russia 102 years earlier for a piddling $7,200,000.

Because of the North Slope strike, the state of Alaska, long a stepchild heavily dependent on federal support, has suddenly become rich. In addition to the bids of almost a billion dollars, the oil companies will be paying large royalties and taxes on their production.

It has been a strange feature of the Alaskan economy that, just when it seems to be sinking into penury, something big and new comes along. First its wealth was in trapping and fishing. Russian fur traders and American salmon canners made their fortunes, but their heyday passed. Then there was the gold rush, but by the eve of World War II placer mining had largely exhausted the pay dirt of the gold fields. The war

Trucks, forced to leave the road at left when it became impassable, have scarred the North Slope.

brought a new boom—and many white settlers—to Alaska, and today the federal government still spends some $750,-000,000 a year on air bases, radar sites, and other installations (the state budget last year was only $155,000,000).

With a billion in the till, Alaskans began to dream. One proposed a new state capital with the Mendenhall Glacier as a backdrop. Another suggested a monorail line to the North Slope. But it was also pointed out that the state was now in a position to treat its native minorities more generously than it had.

Most Americans, vividly familiar with urban ghetto problems nearer home, are unaware of the crisis of the Alaskan Eskimo and other native groups, particularly the Aleuts of the Aleutians and the Athabascan Indians of the interior.

On March 8, 1968, Senator Henry M. Jackson, chairman of the Senate Committee on Interior and Insular Affairs, asked that a special committee look into the land claims of Alaskan natives. The picture painted in the voluminous report of this group is of an ancient culture in agonizing confrontation with modern society. Whereas the Indians of other states endured this crisis a century or more ago, for the Eskimo it is here and now.

In the past sixteen years, during which the Eskimo population has grown 50 per cent, deaths from suicide and alcoholism have doubled. Personality disorders rank third among the causes for hospitalization, second only to accidents (which lead the list and are in part attributed to alcoholism) and respiratory diseases.

Although improved public-health measures have led to an accelerated population growth, infant mortality and adult death rates are double those of white Alaskans. The tuberculosis incidence is twenty times that in the United States as a whole (despite major progress in cutting the rate). One in five Eskimos has never gone to school, and on the North Slope the average resident has not completed fourth grade.

While the ultimate crisis is now, the revolution in North Slope Eskimo life began in 1848 with the entry of New England whalers into the Bering and Chuckchee seas. Traditionally the Tariamiut Eskimos of the coast were long-haul traders as well as hunters of whale, walrus, and seal. Sledding along the coast, they followed trade networks extending from Canada to Siberia; but the whalers soon put them out of business as they transported goods from one village to another.

Apparently because the coastal Eskimos began bartering with the whalers, rather than with the inland Eskimos, the nomadic culture of the latter gradually withered away. Today one of the few remaining inland colonies is that in Anaktuvuk Pass.

Under the impact of white development of their land, Alaskan Eskimos are facing a greatly accelerated change in their traditional way of life. While some, such as the DEW-line cat drivers at Barrow or those working around Prudhoe Bay, have become part of the modern culture, most coastal Eskimos are using the white man's tools to try to continue their old ways. Harpoon guns and rifles have replaced the spear; outboard motorboats have displaced the skin-covered umiak. One even sees an occasional motorcycle leaning against an igloo, and snowmobiles have, in some instances, replaced dog teams.

It is within the family and village that the confrontation is most agonizing. Until the age of seven the typical Eskimo child lives in a home where only Eskimo is spoken. Then he goes to school and has to contend not only with another language but with a completely alien culture. If the student completes high school and comes home, he or she is now an alien in language and in knowledge. The boy is of little use to his father in the latter's struggle to live off the land and has no status among other males of the village. The girl has not learned—or has forgotten—the arts of animal skinning and clothes making.

For many of these young people, graduation from high school has thrust them into a no-man's-land between two cultures. They are unlikely to return to traditional Eskimo life; yet unless they go on to college (and few do), they find it hard to secure jobs in the white man's world. It is understandable why so many Eskimos today turn to drink or suicide.

The immediate issue, of course, is the land-claim situation. The Eskimos do not have a tradition of land ownership. In a state with 375,000,000 acres where, through courage and fortitude, the natives and their ancestors have won a living from an extremely inhospitable land, they own, outright, less than five hundred acres, according to the report to Senator Jackson's committee. All told, 37,400 live in settlements on public domain. In Alaska as a whole, whites now outnumber the natives four to one, but the whites are concentrated in a few centers. Over most of the vastness of Alaskan territory it is the natives that numerically prevail.

Beginning with such incursions as DEW-line construction and Pet 4 exploration, the natives began to organize: by now there are some twenty-one regional and community organizations. In 1966 the statewide Alaska Federation of Natives was organized "to seek an equitable adjustment of Native affairs and Native claims."

The land claims filed by these groups cover about 80 per cent of the state, including some of the richest oil lands. As the North Slope bids were being opened inside the Anchorage auditorium last September, pickets outside carried signs that read: "$2,000,000,000 land robbery" and "Eskimos own North Slope." Leaflets handed out to passers-by said: "Today's lease is perpetrating of economic genocide on a native minority."

When the clamor of the Eskimos reached Washington, Secretary of the Interior Stewart L. Udall called a halt to further release of federal land, pending settlement of the claims issue. President Johnson, in a message to Congress on March 6, 1968, said:

The land rights of the Native people of Alaska —the Aleuts, Eskimos, and Indians—have never been fully or fairly defined. Eighty-four years ago, Congress protected the Alaska Natives in the use and occupancy of their lands. But then, and again when Alaska was given statehood, Congress reserved to itself the power of final decision on ultimate title.

It remains our unfinished task to state in law the terms and conditions of settlement, so that uncertainty can be ended for the Native people of Alaska.

It was two days later that Senator Jackson set in motion a study of the situation. As noted earlier, the resulting report found the situation of the Eskimo

almost catastrophic and recommended a settlement that would set up a corporation, with the natives as shareholders, to conduct educational and development projects. The Jackson committee modified this scheme, proposing two corporations: the Alaska Native Services Corporation and the Alaska Native Investment Corporation. Two per cent of federal income from mineral and oil leases would go to these native-owned corporations until the total reached $500,000,000.

An alternate proposal by the Interior Department would involve a flat payment of $500,000,000 to the natives. Incidentally, Walter Hickel, when he was governor of Alaska, revealed his impatience with the land freeze imposed by Udall, which he felt was throttling the state's development. Since he was known to have extensive business interests in Alaska, Hickel was closely questioned by the Senate Interior Committee during hearings on his nomination as Secretary of the Interior, and he pledged to continue the freeze until this year.

But by January of 1970, with the oil companies clamoring for permission to build a giant pipeline from the North Slope to the south coast of Alaska, Hickel had lowered the barriers in two respects. He had given permission for construction of an all-year road for hauling pipeline materials to the Yukon, and he had set the stage for releasing land along the pipeline route, once the engineering plans had been finally approved.

The pipeline project is one of two apparently feasible solutions to the greatest problem facing the oil companies: getting the oil out to populated areas. The second solution is the use of giant tankers to bully their way through the Arctic ice.

Humble Oil assigned its 1,005-foot *Manhattan* to test the sea route. This, the largest tanker flying the American flag, was cut into four sections so that modification work could proceed at maximum speed. Eventually all parts, including a new bow, were brought together and reassembled.

On August 24, 1969, the ship left Delaware Bay with a group that included seventy-two scientists, oil company representatives, Canadian officials, and newsmen. Its bow, reaching ahead like the neck of a flying waterfowl, was aimed

north. The ship sailed between Greenland and Baffin Island and turned west to fight its way through the ice-clogged channels of the Arctic Archipelago in the hope of achieving what so many earlier mariners had attempted—the Northwest Passage.

The ship, displacing 150,000 tons and with engines developing 42,000 horsepower, plowed its way through the ice as no ship ever had before. But when it was first brought to a dead halt, off Melville Island, on September 9, its weakness also became apparent. The bulk of this monster was so enormous that, once dead in the water, it was hard to get it moving again, particularly if the ice pressed close, leaving no room to back and charge. The final frustration came in McClure Strait, and the giant ship had to give up and take a detour around Banks Island.

On September 14 it broke through the ice into open water that stretched as far as the sailors could see toward the Alaskan coast. While small exploration ships and a Canadian icebreaker had made the Northwest Passage since Sir John Franklin's ill-fated attempts, this was the first commercial ship to do so. A week later it arrived off Point Barrow, to be greeted by Secretary Hickel and other officials. (The *Manhattan* could not reach Prudhoe Bay because of shallow water, and, in fact, if tankers are used to haul out the oil, some sort of staging system will be necessary.)

Meanwhile, throughout 1969, preparations for construction of the Trans-Alaska Pipeline Systems, or TAPS, went forward, even though the Interior Department had not yet granted permission for the project (which would require making an exception to the general freeze on land allocations). When Secretary Hickel authorized the TAPS oil companies to build an all-year road from Livengood to the Yukon so that pipe for the project could be hauled that far north, he remarked that "the performance on this road construction will bear direct relevance to our subsequent response to the eight-hundred-mile pipeline application." The road was the first leg of a projected 390-mile all-year link to Prudhoe Bay.

The pipeline will be mammoth, with a four-foot girth. The eight hundred miles of pipe are being imported from Japan.

With pumping stations, terminal facilities, and access roads it will cost some $900,000,000. TAPS was originally a consortium of Atlantic-Richfield, BP, and Humble, but more companies have joined in. They hoped to have the oil flowing by 1972. However, legal action initiated by conservation groups led to the issuance, on April 13, 1970, of a federal court order enjoining Hickel from issuing a right-of-way permit for extending the road from the Yukon to Prudhoe Bay, pending settlement of a dispute on right-of-way width and further assessment of the environmental effects.

Of the many formidable problems raised by this project the most serious arise from the high temperature of the oil—and hence of the pipe itself. The oil, heated in the bowels of the earth, comes out of the ground at about 160°, and, from the friction of its high-speed flow through the pipe and the energy introduced by pumping, it may be even hotter when it reaches Valdez at its southern terminus.

Thus, if the pipe were laid directly on permafrost, it would melt itself into the ground, forming a giant trench and causing severe erosion. Where there were wedges of ice in otherwise solid ground, a cavity would form under the pipe which could produce a rupture. With 500,000 gallons of fast-moving oil in every mile of pipe, such a rupture would deluge the landscape. On a slope, a sudden mudflow could carry away part of the pipe, producing the same effect. To reach Valdez the pipe must cross the Fairweather Fault, where slippage produced one of the most violent earthquakes of modern times, bringing Anchorage down in ruins and causing severe damage in Valdez.

The obvious route for the line, insofar as possible, is along rivers where the permafrost lies deep and gravel for insulation is plentiful. But a break there could have particularly disastrous effects. A spill along the proposed route of the pipe beside the Dietrich River, after it has crossed the 4,650-foot Dietrich Pass, would send oil rushing down that stream and ultimately, via the Yu-

U.S. OIL POLICY AND THE ENVIRONMENT

In a recent report Secretary of the Interior Walter Hickel, among others, argued in support of the government's current program limiting the amount of low-cost foreign oil allowed into this country by pointing out that "At the world market price of oil, [Alaskan] exploration and development would have been unlikely." The statement also mentioned that "billions of barrels of oil . . . on offshore leases have been developed as the result of the economic incentives preserved by the [import] controls. At substantially lower oil prices this development would not have occurred."

As the conservative economist Milton Friedman has written, "Few industries sing the praises of free enterprise more loudly than the oil industry. Yet few industries rely so heavily on special government favors." The special government favors started in 1926 with a percentage depletion allowance that exempted from taxation a whopping 27½ per cent (reduced last year to 22 per cent) of gross income from oil wells, up to 50 per cent of net income. The allowance can be deducted through the entire life of the oil well, even after all costs have been met. The depletion allowance encouraged excessive production and led in the early 1930's to a system of state-controlled production rationing based on market demand. The resulting high-cost domestic oil was further protected (in the name of national defense) from the competition of cheaper foreign oil by the introduction in 1959 of an import quota system.

The recent intensive scrutiny of government oil policy—through the presidential task force on the oil-import question, Senate Judiciary Antitrust and Monopoly Subcommittee hearings, Senate debate on the depletion allowance—has focused only on the economic ramifications of that policy and on the question of national self-sufficiency from a military point of view. The question of what might constitute an environmentally rational oil policy has hardly been raised, except by a few conservationists such as Malcolm Baldwin, a lawyer with the Conservation Foundation.

We are told by the petroleum industry that domestic demand for oil will nearly double by 1985, while at the same time our domestic supplies are growing short, and the largest source of foreign oil, the Middle East, is politically unstable. What options do we have? If we leave Alaskan oil in the ground does it mean we must risk more offshore disasters like the ones at Santa Barbara and, more recently, in Louisiana? Or would we be better off building more and bigger ships for Middle Eastern, offshore Nigerian, Libyan, or Venezuelan oil and risking even more terrifying *Torrey Canyon* episodes and more frequent pollution of the oceans? If we chose this course, we would be creating the need for larger ports (such as that proposed for Machiasport, Maine, and opposed by conservationists), more dredging of vital, life-supporting estuaries, more onshore receiving facilities. As Mr. Baldwin has pointed out, Congress has, in fact, already unwittingly encouraged the building of more 200,-000-to-500,000-ton supertankers by recently limiting shipping liability to fourteen million dollars for an oil-spill disaster, although legitimate claims after the relatively small *Torrey Canyon* wreck were over sixteen million dollars.

Moreover, should our oil policy offer inducements to import foreign oil, such as Libyan oil, that is low in sulphur content? (Alaskan oil also has a low sulphur content.) Should the oil-shale reserves in the wild and beautiful plateau country of Colorado, Wyoming, and Utah be opened up? Oil-shale reserves represent a supply three times as large as the known crude petroleum reserves in the entire world and are low in sulphur as well.

Basically, a rational oil policy would be one that regards oil (like earth itself) as a limited commodity whose use and distribution should be managed only with regard to other possible energy sources. It would be a policy that looks ahead to a time when more petroleum either cannot be made available, or should not, simply out of regard for the environment and man's future. —*E.N.L.*

kon, to the sea.

This would affect spawning beds, waterfowl breeding areas, and the entire wildlife regime of the area. Another danger is disturbance of the spawning beds either by upstream silting during construction or by destruction of the beds themselves through removal of their gravel. Salmon and arctic char fight their long upstream battles to lay their eggs on flat gravel beds beneath clear-flowing water.

Another concern has been the effect of the pipeline as a barrier to caribou migrations. For a considerable distance the pipeline will be carried across permafrost areas on stilts. A pipe four feet in diameter standing on two-foot stilts would be a formidable obstacle to the caribou. Undisturbed northward movement of the herds in spring is vital to their survival since, in order to reach the calving grounds when the young are born, they must cross the mountain passes before the snow gets soft. Otherwise the calves are dropped too early and abandoned.

Since the rivers themselves present ever-changing obstacles to migration, the animals may learn to bypass such an impediment. Early fears that their movements would be disturbed by roads and other such works of man seem unfounded: herds have moved freely across airstrips and, in dark periods, some even have been known to rest on drill pads. It may also be possible, at natural crossing points, to raise the pipe enough to permit the passage of herds.

Bears, among other animals, are finding their life pattern disturbed by the incursions of the oil companies, but they seem to be taking a certain amount of counteraction on their own. I was told of an emergency situation that arose at a scientific station on an ice floe large enough to accommodate a ski-plane landing strip. A supply plane was en route during the polar night, and when the switch was thrown to turn on the runway lights, nothing happened. The men, warmly bundled, checked the line of lights and found, from tracks in the snow, that a polar bear had systematically gone up the runway swatting each light with his paw.

Because of such incursions, oil prospecting teams are often armed. Bears are easy marks on the open terrain, and so many have been shot that this spring

the grizzly hunting season was closed.

In the foothills the barren ground grizzly has upset the best-laid plans of oil prospectors and others. He will break into a food cache and bite into each can, sucking out the contents. In one case of which I was told some of the cans contained gasoline, and one was full of smoke bombs used to indicate wind direction to arriving bush pilots. Apparently one of the bombs went off when the bear bit into it, and the bear ran amok, tearing a tent to ribbons and hurling boxes for fifty yards in all directions.

The planned route of the pipe from the Dietrich Pass is across (or more probably under) the Yukon to Fairbanks, and then down the highway system to Valdez. The Interior Department has produced two book-sized volumes of stipulations for approval of TAPS. They include the posting of a $5,000,000 bond against damage done by spills, and the presence of federal monitors with construction crews to see that they do not excessively damage the terrain. Also, the pipeline must go under streams unless otherwise authorized by the Interior Department, and detailed contingency plans must be made in case of spills.

In April the oil companies, which had hoped to start work on the pipeline this summer, suffered a setback. The United States Geological Survey advised Secretary Hickel that the pipeline plan, as presently constituted, did not give adequate assurance that the environment would be protected. In particular, said the specialists, it was evident that the pipe should not be buried along most of the route, as was the intent of the TAPS project. It was estimated that the pipe would melt the ground to a depth of fifty feet, converting frozen silt into an impassable canal. At least 40 per cent of the 800-mile pipe would have to be above the ground, the experts said. This, plus the legal actions of pipeline opponents, indicated a delay of at least a year.

Once the line is built, some Alaskan conservationists fear the state will not pay much attention to oil spills and other insults to the environment. They note that in Cook Inlet, where since 1965 there have been more than 150 recorded spills from offshore rigs, tankers, barges, and the like, only five violators were prosecuted. The state, when Hickel was

governor, enacted unusually strict anti-pollution laws; but personnel to enforce them are in short supply.

One of the most sobering bits of ecological news last year was a report from the Woods Hole Oceanographic Institution in Massachusetts that global oil spillage has reached the point where even little-travelled waters in mid-ocean are coated with scum. One of the few oceans largely spared such pollution has been the Arctic. But what if a tanker like the *Manhattan*—or one of the proposed far larger type—is punctured by ice?

Some have suggested that such an oil spill could blacken the polar ice sufficiently to cause its melting, bringing about a change of local climate that would tip the scales of global air currents and produce a new ice age—probably a farfetched idea; but such a spill would have profound effects on the fragile balance of life in the Arctic.

In an introduction to one of Bob Marshall's books Professor A. Starker Leopold, of the University of California, wrote: "It is characteristic of frontier societies, and Alaska still is such, to become so engrossed in the process of development as to fail to look ahead to the point of diminishing returns beyond which more development becomes a social liability rather than an asset."

Marshall himself argued that "If Alaska were to remain primarily a great reservoir of resources, largely untapped at present, but available for future use, it would seem as if that balance which should be a major feature of sound planning would best be realized."

A critical issue in this respect is whether the world's oil reserves will last until alternate sources of power have been developed. Current progress toward development of fusion reactors that would tame the power of the hydrogen bomb has led many to predict that by the end of the century we will be free from overwhelming dependence on oil as our energy source.

Recent offshore exploration north of Alaska and the Canadian oil strike at the mouth of the Mackenzie also indicate that extensive oil deposits lie in that vast region. The extension of continental structure—the so-called continental shelf of shallow water—fringing Alaska is as large as the state itself. Of all continental shelf along United States shores, half is off Alaska.

Thus plenty of oil seems to be there. One can argue that were it not for the subsidy of American producers by means of import restrictions, it would not be economical to exploit at this time.

"Only with the continuation of a reasonable import control program," said Rawleigh Warner, Jr., chairman of Mobil, early in 1970, "will it be economically desirable for oil companies to continue their search for additional reserves in remote and difficult areas such as this." A similar view has been expressed by Michael L. Haider, chairman of Standard of New Jersey, who predicted that Alaskan oil will not be able to compete with Middle Eastern oil on world markets.

There is little doubt, however, that the imports of competitive oil will continue to be controlled, and that North Slope exploitation will proceed. The great responsibility of the American people and their government, therefore, is to see that the oil is extracted without destroying this continent's last great wilderness.

The life of the North Slope and its fringing seas is not precious merely for sentimental reasons. It is of great biological importance. The manner in which these life forms have adapted to a harsh environment is unique. It is the fruit of millions of years of slow evolution. The lessons that these plants and animals can teach us for our own survival and welfare are many, but some of these organisms could be completely wiped out in a decade.

As a single example, Dr. Laurence Irving, of the University of Alaska, cites a warbler that winters in a certain spot in Venezuela, then migrates through the Anaktuvuk Pass to find, "with the accuracy of an intercontinental missile," its nesting place on the North Slope. The warbler's weight of ten grams, he points out, "contains the entire machinery for guidance of its navigation, for its memory and operation in flight, and for determining its initiation."

What a loss to all humanity—and all nature—if such a creature were wiped out by careless tampering with the environment!

The face of the land could also be altered radically. If the tundra is destroyed

and the muddy ice that underlies it melts and flows away, the surface in many areas will be below sea level. It would then not be long before Alaskan territory would be correspondingly reduced.

This, then, is a great challenge to American wisdom and ingenuity. There is no doubt but that the oil companies are trying to meet it. "Don't you like your stockholders?" said Dr. Max Brewer, head of the Naval Arctic Research Laboratory, as he showed a photograph of Prudhoe Bay State No. 1, immersed in a mud field, to an oil company man. His point was that it is far more economical to make the initial investment and insulate the permafrost.

The oil companies reportedly have now agreed among themselves not to move equipment across the tundra during the four or five months of the summer thaw. They are using air-cushioned hovercraft and the big helicopters known as flying cranes to hop from one site to another. Two drill rigs that can be broken down into eighteen-thousand-pound units were ferried across the tundra last summer in this way, although one flying crane crashed disastrously.

The oilmen are also planning to drill four to six wells from a single pad, boring obliquely to cover a 640-acre sector of the oil reservoir. This will reduce both cost, in terms of pad construction, and disturbance of the tundra. Atlantic-Richfield and Humble have built a two-hundred-man camp at Prudhoe at a cost of $7,500,000, of which $2,000,000 was for the sewage and water-supply system. Both are a major challenge in a permafrost region.

From the days of the first European settlers the American tradition has been one of conquest—conquest of hostile tribes, of a hostile environment, and of vast distances. As pointed out by Starker Leopold, this spirit persists. It is reflected in the indignant comment of Alaska's Senator Ted Stevens, who dismissed the Interior Department's pipeline stipulations as "stupid, absolutely stupid."

"Alaskans know Alaska," he told the Alaska Science Conference in 1969. "I'm fed up to here with people who try to tell us how to develop our country."

"Tomorrow," said Alaska's Governor Keith H. Miller on the eve of the great 1969 lease sale, "we will reach out to claim our birthright. We will ren-

dezvous with our dreams."

A more sensitive expression of that pioneer spirit was written by Robert W. Service:

I am the land that listens, I am the land
*   that broods;*
Steeped in eternal beauty, crystalline
*   waters and woods . . .*
Wild and wide are my borders, stern as
*   death is my sway,*
And I wait for the men who will win me—
*   and I will not be won in a day.*

Today we stand face-to-face with the Arctic Ocean. The North Slope is the end of the line for American conquest—the North Slope and the moon.

It has been argued that it is more difficult for us, with our Judaeo-Christian tradition, to live in harmony with nature than it is for those raised in Asiatic cultures. As noted by Philip Johnson, an ecologist with the Army's Cold Regions Research and Engineering Laboratory, at the conference on North Slope ecology last year, the Garden of Eden typifies the view of a world made for our benefit. The dominant attitude of our culture, Dr. Johnson said, "is egocentric about man and exploitive about nature."

Yet, as he pointed out, any species that overwhelms its environment invites destruction. Such a species either exhausts its food supply or becomes so prolific that some devastating predator evolves to devour it. We have evaded this law of nature so far but cannot do so indefinitely.

Perhaps, in this respect, we should not forget what the Eskimo says to us: "Take your planes, and cars, and washing machines, and supermarkets. Throw them all away and I can still live. Even on the Arctic pack, I can live."

There are anthropologists who believe the Eskimo and his culture will survive the present onslaught. The Arctic, they say, is too harsh for normal settlement by the white man, but it will always be able to support Eskimos in the traditional manner.

If we can save the Arctic for the Eskimos, perhaps we can save the rest of the continent for ourselves.

Mr. Sullivan, the distinguished science editor of the New York Times, *has won many awards for his own writing on science.*

THE ENVIRONMENT:

Notes on the continuing battle   *By* ELIZABETH N. LAYNE

MINING THE PUBLIC LANDS

The Mining Act of 1866 declared "the mineral lands of the public domain . . . free and open to exploration and occupation," and to this day it is perfectly legal for any citizen to seek his fortune on the public lands. Not only are "vacant" unappropriated lands at the miners' disposal but also areas set aside for other uses, such as national forests and wildlife ranges and refuges that were carved out of lands originally part of the public domain. Even some national monuments and one national park can be mined. Congress has made mining legal in Mount McKinley National Park and Glacier Bay National Monument in Alaska, Organ Pipe Cactus National Monument in Arizona, and Death Valley National Monument in California. Such is the power of the mining lobby that although the Wilderness Act of 1964 created a unique system of wilderness preserves to be protected from all development (no roads, no structures), it also permitted those preserves to remain open to mineral exploitation until 1984.

Under the antiquated general mining laws the miner need only establish sufficient "mineralization" to stake a claim on public land; he is not required to notify the federal government of its location, nor need he obtain a permit to operate. Nothing in these laws controls his operations or requires any restoration or treatment of "disturbed" land. Federal laws, in fact, not only permit mining on the public lands, but they also foster mineral development by providing loans amounting to 50 per cent of exploration costs; the loans are repayable only if the mine is a success. The miner can, by a relatively simple process, obtain a patent to his claim that gives him ownership of the property. Patent owners then have every right to build resort hotels, subdivide the land, or cut down the timber.

The Federal Leasing Act of 1920 stipulates that certain minerals, such as oil, coal, and phosphate, cannot be mined without a lease from the Secretary of the Interior. But aside from that, the balance is as much in favor of mineral development on public lands today as it was in 1908, when Theodore Roosevelt hurriedly declared the Grand Canyon a "national monument" (and closed to mining) in order to keep the magnifi-

Open-pit molybdenum mining like that in New Mexico (directly above) is now being planned for Idaho's spectacular Castle Peak (top).

cent canyon out of the hands of a speculator. Grand Canyon was then still part of the public domain, and the speculator, seeing its tourist potential, had sought to control access by staking out mining claims along the rim.

Striking evidence of the need today for mining-law reform lies at the base of Castle Peak in Idaho's White Cloud Mountains in Challis National Forest. The White Clouds form a small wilderness area of seventy square miles domi-

nated by snow-dusted Castle Peak, which rises to 11,820 feet above alpine lakes and meadows. The lakes are rich in rainbow and cutthroat trout; the meadows and mountain slopes are a sanctuary for elk, mountain goats, and bighorn sheep. Castle Peak waters drain into the East Fork of the Salmon River, prime spawning grounds for the beleaguered chinook salmon. It is a roadless area, and the U.S. Forest Service planned to keep it that way.

Yet wildcat prospectors are bulldozing in search of minerals, and in the summer of 1968 the American Smelting and Refining Company (ASARCO) staked out molybdenum claims at the base of Castle Peak. (Molybdenum is an alloy used primarily to harden steel and is in abundant supply in this nation.) Plans were made for an open-pit mine, expected to produce twenty thousand tons of ore a day from a pit covering nearly five million square feet. Initial samples from test drillings showed a molybdenum concentration of two tenths of one per cent. In other words, 99.8 per cent of the excavated rock from the open-pit mine would be waste sludge. An estimated annual accumulation of seven million tons of waste would be piled in the meadows, and, according to the regional office of the U.S. Bureau of Sport Fisheries and Wildlife, this would pollute the waters of the salmon spawning grounds. ASARCO's discovery attracted other miners to the White Clouds, and claims are now spotted everywhere. At this writing, conservationists are moving in two directions to preserve the area. The National Wildlife Federation is hoping to challenge the legality of the operations in court, while the Greater Sawtooth Preservation Council, a local group led by economics professor John Merriam of Idaho State University, is pushing for the protection of national-park status.

Although congressmen have proposed legislation calling for a system under which leases would be required from all mining interests seeking to operate in the public lands, reform of the laws cannot come in time to save the White Clouds. Only conservation efforts can do that.

THE BIG RACE

"Easy Rider" Reid

The internal-combustion engine causes more than 60 per cent of all air pollution in our cities. Ride a bicycle to work instead of driving a car and you help make a cleaner, quieter, more pleasant city to live in. One champion of the bicycle as the urban commuter's best friend is the twenty-five-year-old son of a Detroit automobile executive, Lieutenant (j.g.) Thomas R. Reid III. The U.S. Navy set the wheels of revolution in motion when they plucked Mr. Reid from his teaching post (Greek) at Johns Hopkins University and put him behind a desk in downtown Washington four miles from where he found a place to live. Reid quickly discovered that the fastest, cheapest, "most fun way" to get to work—rain or shine—was on his bike. In order to prove this to a skeptical world, he staged a race last fall from his home to the District Building, where he works. He pitted himself and his two-wheeler against a driver in a Porsche sports car and a commuter on a city bus. Mr. Reid won hands down: the driver arrived three minutes behind the cyclist and even then had to park illegally before dashing across the finish line; the bus rider trailed by fourteen minutes.

The ivory-tower theorist behind Reid's fancy footwork is Dr. Wilcomb Washburn, head of the Division of American Studies at the Smithsonian Institution. Dr. Washburn has long proposed the establishment of commuter bicycle routes, and last summer his department produced a comprehensive plan for Washington. Reid's unique race was part of an effort to convince the city that the plan deserved serious consideration. Since then Washington has seen these changes on behalf of the cyclist:

• The city council has implemented the first stage of the Smithsonian plan by establishing three well-marked bicycle routes into the Federal Triangle in downtown Washington, where 70 per cent of the government's employees work.

• The General Services Administration is supplying bicycle racks for twenty-five government buildings.

• The Washington police promise to put up posters warning drivers to watch out for cyclists. The traffic commission will mark a bike lane on designated routes with a serrated red line to show cyclists where they can and should go.

• Fifteen miles of four-lane highway through Rock Creek Park in the heart of the city are now closed to Sunday automobile traffic, and a path for bike commuters will be built through the park.

Reid and his activist associates, lawyer Donald Green and Clay Grubic, an ex-C.I.A. man who now runs a bike shop, are urging the District to expand its use of the Smithsonian plan. They want the District to designate more routes for bike commuters and for tourists, to allow adult cyclists on sidewalks in such highly dangerous areas as bridges, and to build more special bike paths along particularly busy roads.

A QUESTION OF VALUES

South Street, as old as Philadelphia itself, is the southernmost rung of William Penn's ladder of streets spanning the land between the Delaware and the Schuylkill rivers. It is the commercial heart of one of this country's oldest black communities, made famous by Dr. W. E. B. Du Bois' 1897 sociological study of the Philadelphia Negro for the University of Pennsylvania. The street is a ribbon of small shops and houses that ties together a whole neighborhood and keeps the community viable. It is a street of beautiful nineteenth-century storefronts, "unique, urbanistically eloquent in their relation to sidewalk and street," in the words of city planner Denise Venturi.

South Street has been slated for demolition for fifteen years. The city plans eight lanes of concrete cross-town expressway along its length, a flowing moat of automobiles between the blacks of South Philadelphia and the middle-class whites of Society Hill and Rittenhouse Square. A community can't hold its breath for fifteen years while a city sorts out its problems, and one third of South Street rots as it waits. But the community that remains has a loud and effective voice: a citizens' committee led by Mrs. Alice Lipscomb, who has been joined by the civic-minded and the concerned of the white community—the Society Hill Civic Association, a lawyer named Robert Sugarman, the planning firm of Venturi and Rauch, and many more. Together they hope to convince Mayor James Tate, the Chamber of Commerce, and the last of several study groups to kill once and for all the cross-town expressway and let South Street renew itself.

THE VACATIONIST

Our nation's motorists litter the highways with 1,304 pieces of trash over each mile every month, according to a survey made for America the Beautiful, Inc., by the National Academy of Sciences.

The American Heritage Society Awards

The February issue of AMERICAN HERITAGE announced that the American Heritage Society would divide $50,000 in "seed money" awards among twelve local, nonprofit groups that are working to save some part of America's endangered physical heritage.

The twelve were chosen with the counsel of our two sponsors, the American Association for State and Local History and the Society of American Historians, and a number of conservation experts. While any such selection is bound to be somewhat arbitrary, we tried to spread the locales and the nature of the projects broadly.

Then we asked here for postcard votes from our Society members and other readers. And we mailed ballots to a wide cross-section of others who we believed are interested in conservation. To make sure no one really lost, we promised a minimum award of $1,000 to each group. The votes were to determine which four organizations would receive the larger awards of $25,000, $10,000, $5,000, and $2,000. A total of 114,146 voters ranked the groups in this order:

(1) Alaska Conservation Society, College, Alaska $25,000

(2) Big Thicket Association, Liberty, Texas $10,000

(3) Scenic Hudson Preservation Conference, New York, New York $5,000

(4) Hells Canyon Preservation Council, Idaho Falls, Idaho $2,000

(5) Laughing Brook Education Center, Hampden, Massachusetts $1,000

(6) Delaware Valley Citizens' Council for Clean Air, Philadelphia, Pennsylvania $1,000

(7) Sanibel-Captiva Conservation Foundation, Inc., Sanibel Island, Florida $1,000

(8) Conservation Society of Southern Vermont, Bondville, Vermont $1,000

(9) The Old Santa Fe Association, Santa Fe, New Mexico $1,000

(10) South Hill Neighborhood Association, Lexington, Kentucky $1,000

(11) Escalante Wilderness Committee, Salt Lake City, Utah $1,000

(12) The Wyckoff Association in America, Brooklyn, New York $1,000

By sheer coincidence, AMERICAN HERITAGE had already arranged, months before the balloting ended, to publish the long article on Alaska by Walter Sullivan that appears on pages 98–117. It is thus possible for interested readers to gain some insights into the problems facing that giant state and the winner of our major award, to whom we extend our congratulations.

To all who voted, our thanks for making the decisions for the Society. All the twelve groups tell us that even $1,000 is an encouraging windfall—enough to hire a lawyer, print a pamphlet, run an ad. In any event, the Society hopes the awards may provide some balm for our injured land and heritage.